GARDEN
ALPINES

GARDEN
ALPINES

ALAN BLOOM

AIDAN ELLIS

First published in the United Kingdom
by Aidan Ellis Publishing, Cobb House,
Nuffield, Henley-on-Thames, Oxon RG9 5RT

First edition 1994

A CIP catalogue record for this book
is available from the British Library
ISBN 0 85628 254 5

Designed by Craig Dodd

Page make-up and typesetting by
Contour Typesetters, Southall, Middx UB2 4BD

Text film and colour reproduction by
J Film Process Co Ltd.

Printed in Italy by
Vincenzo Bona srl, Turin

Frontispiece: Aquilegia discolor

CONTENTS

Alan Bloom's addiction to alpines began in 1923 when helping on his father's market garden at Oakington near Cambridge. This he converted into a hardy plant nursery in 1931, and by 1938 it covered thirty-six acres and included 200,000 alpines. Some new varieties he raised during that period are still popular. Moving to Bressingham in 1946, even greater production was reached, still wholesale only; but since 1965 retailing also under the name Bressingham Gardens has brought much greater publicity. Alan Bloom has to a large extent pioneered both 'island beds' for perennials, and raised beds rather than 'rockeries' for alpines. Most of his books have been on how to make the best use of the fascinating range of perennials and alpines.

His previous books include *A Plantsman's Perspective* and *Hardy Perennials*

INTRODUCTION

The use of the word 'alpine' for the plants of garden value does not mean they all originate from the Alps. Neither does it mean that all come from other mountainous regions. For lack of a better term, it is merely a convenient word to describe the vast group of low dwarf, or slow growing plants which can effectively be used in gardens. The term 'rockery', or rock garden plants, is inadequate because very few in this group need rocks between which to grow. The majority are very adaptable, with regard to both soil and climate. This book deals with alpines which are both winter-hardy and perennial. Annuals, along with many dwarf, bulbous subjects are excluded because they are seldom compatible with the wide and more interesting range of perennials. These are more satisfying to grow, and my general list of recommendations is almost entirely made up of kinds which are reliable in a wide variety of situations. And I must emphasise that an artificially made rockery, or rock garden, is not the only, nor necessarily the best, place in which to grow alpines. One of the main objectives of this book is to describe the various ways in which alpine plants can be grown to good effect, and with the minimum of trouble and after-care.

Historical background

The cultivation of alpine plants is a relatively new practice, which arose chiefly from the explorations of the past two hundred years. The explorers, who were often botanists, brought back large collections of newly-discovered plants mainly to Europe from the wild. Among these plants were small as well as tall growing kinds, and of course trees and shrubs. The latter were easier to place in botanic and other gardens, but the small ones needed a place to themselves, where they would not be overshadowed or invaded.

It was, therefore, natural to choose a site where they could be fully seen and appreciated. And because many had been found where rock formations abounded, or were from high altitudes, nineteenth century gardeners introduced rocks to enhance the plants. Since the European Alps were the first to be explored, the terms 'rockery' or 'rock garden' came into use along with 'alpines' for the whole range of plants. Very few true rock gardens existed before 1900. Although by then the so-called 'rockery' was becoming a popular feature, it was often ridiculously exaggerated and quite out of keeping, both aesthetically and for the welfare of all but the more robust kinds. Usually it consisted of a mound of earth, often in an obscure or shady situation, on which lumps of stone were dotted with no regard to beauty or suitability. Between the stones were spaces called 'pockets' for the plants, but so often the choicer ones died in such harsh, unnatural conditions. And the mound itself was often difficult to weed or water, which meant that only the more rampant ones survived and took possession.

The 'rockery' still survives in cases where garden owners know no better – sometimes even lumps of concrete are used as a substitute for rocks. In gardens far away from rocky or hilly areas, placing rocks in an imitation of mountain scenery is out of place. There are other, better means of growing alpines in flat or formal gardens which are described later on in this book.

Categories of alpine plants

As a generalisation, it is safe to say that the most successful gardens are those where the plants grown are naturally suited or adaptable to the prevailing conditions of soil, situation and climate. And this certainly applies to the cultivation of alpine plants. Although so many are adaptable, it stands to reason that those native to high alpine screes and moraines will need conditions different from those inhabiting woods, meadows, tundra or sandy banks at low altitudes. And the same applies to latitudes, where their long-standing habitat has put limits on their moisture requirement and degree of hardiness.

It follows on evolutionary principles that, as plants adapt themselves to the prevailing conditions in nature, the habit of growth shows wide variations. The term 'habit' has become accepted for describing the type of growth, and in alpines this falls into several sections.

From the highest altitudes and high rock places, come most of those with a slow growth rate, and they are also often of low hummock, or cushion formation, with minute leaves or rosettes. These are known as scree plants, needing very little soil, but very good drainage. They are found growing at altitudes well over 1,000 metres, where they may be under snow from October to May. But they remain relatively dry over this long period as little or no moisture soaks down to their roots until the snow begins to melt. Then, as summer comes, one can see the thrilling, almost miraculous, sight of flowers peering through the remaining snow. It is the short period of growth, with cold nights, which has made such plants so diminutive; and they remain so in gardens, despite more favourable climatic conditions where they may spread more quickly if it is in their nature to do so.

As might be expected, these high altitude alpines are the most difficult to adapt to garden conditions, as they need gritty soil but object to both winter and summer drought and heat. They are often grown to good advantage in stone sinks and troughs; but some are best in what is known as an alpine house, where the glass covering keeps off winter wet and where moisture requirements can be met in summer.

Because of their special needs, not so many scree plants are mentioned in the list of recommendations, but the variety avail-able is so wide that a number of cushion-forming plants which are less fussy are included.

Another habit group is those plants which have a bushy, semi-shrubby formation. This may be upright or more spreading, and evergreen or deciduous as far as foliage is concerned, but comes from a more or less central root, with life retained above ground over winter regardless of whether foliage is lost. These are described as of a bushy or trailing habit, and are generally easy to grow. Examples of the erect and bushy type are seen in *Iberis*, *Helianthemum*, *Gypsophila* and some of the trailing *Penstemon*.

In the wild, most bush-forming alpines are found on hills and mountains bordering on the Mediterranean, or in the Near and Middle East. In these areas, summers are hot and dry but, when roots can penetrate deeply or into rock crevices and walls, plants can survive. Unlike those growing in a mild, moist climate, leaves hold very little sap, which is often an indication of a low rainfall and a short rainy season. It is in this short season that new growth and flowering takes place. This range of plants will often flourish in gardens, but may need trimming to keep shapely and neat.

Other groups having individual growth habits include those of mat-like growth. These (together with carpeters) often root down into the soil as they spread with varying rapidity, and more often than not keep themselves clothed over winter. Some smother themselves with flowers in summer, but others are grown purely for their silvery and green foliage. These are useful plants and are amongst the easiest to grow: they include such well-known subjects as *Aubrieta*, alpine phlox and thymes.

One other important type is those which die down in true herbaceous character, to a

Overleaf: Rock Garden, Frog Hall

live, but scarcely visible, rootstock during winter dormacy. They are often found in alpine meadows or anywhere with a fair depth of soil. Because of competition with other plants, including grasses, in a natural habitat they survive by sharing that habitat. Some associate with plants which have a different root system, allowing roots to feed at different levels. Other grow at different heights and share air and light. And it is interesting that as a result some plants will grow better in association with others.

Alpines may also be clump-forming, which means that they do not spread by underground shoots when they expand in size. The large genus of *Campanula* includes some with this habit. Others with this habit of spreading underground can be a nuisance as they invade neighbouring plants. The general descriptive list mentions any species with this habit, and those plants with a rampant nature; and advice is given later on how best to avoid harmful competition. It should be noted that rampant means rapid spread above ground, and invasive refers to spread below the surface. Naturally, there are some alpines which fall between the two, which emphasises the variety in habit of growth, as well as in the range of adaptability and uses to which the plants can be put. There are alpines suitable for almost any position in a garden, but the vast majority prefer an open, sunny position, well-drained but not too deprived of moisture. The most difficult site for growing alpines, as with taller herbaceous or border plants, is dry shade under trees where the roots starve the soil, and where low, overhanging branches keep off sunlight and air.

For those who wish to grow alpines for their beauty, the first consideration must be to decide on a suitable site. If there are restrictions in the choice of site, then preparations should be made to give the plants the best possible chance and to choose plants which will adapt.

Ways and means to grow alpines

A suitable site can be found in most gardens where a pleasing selection of plants can be grown successfully. The ideal, and most common, is an open position, with a fair amount of sunlight, which will accommodate the widest and most colourful range. With a flat or gently sloping garden with no natural rock formation, a decision must be made whether to use rocks at all. A clumsily, or unskilfully, constructed rockery or rock garden can spoil the overall design. And it can prove an expensive outlay, difficult to maintain and restrictive if the rocks take up too much space or are badly spaced. This is not to decry the use of rocks, but merely to encourage the garden owner to think carefully before introducing them. Some people may feel that alpines without rocks are incongruous, and it is a matter of personal choice. But one of the most glaring examples of a badly constructed rock garden I remember seeing was a three-metre high 'Matterhorn' built by an alpine enthusiast as the focal point. My own belief is that, if one wishes to grow alpines for their beauty, it is best to limit the use of rocks to easing slopes or to gently breaking up any tendency to flatness in the garden.

There are many situations where alpines can be grown without the extravagant use of rocks. But, as so many kinds are diminutive, it is worth considering making a raised bed especially for them. Unless the ground has sufficient natural slope to form a terrace or bank, this involves building a low wall. And a low wall is also needed with terracing where a slope is already steep enough to allow erosion to take place, or so slight that a bed cannot be raised without one. If there is no objection to bending down, an alternative is to have a 'walkabout bed'. This can be made by using stone or bricks around the perimeter and filling in with a suitable soil mixture. It is easy to arrange access with flat stones or bricks to tread on.

Terracing, raised and 'walkabout' beds are all covered separately below, together with large or small rock gardens and detailed advice on preparation, construction and maintenance.

The importance of drainage

The first essential for all methods is to ensure good drainage and this is largely dependent on the existing type of soil. In most cases, the nature of the topsoil is in turn determined by the subsoil. If this is sand or gravel, the topsoil will be light and drainage no problem. But a heavy topsoil, hard when dry and sticky when wet, usually indicates clay as being the subsoil. Clays may vary from chalky marl to the tough, grey-blue or yellowish type, but all are resistent to water to some extext and liable to impede water if consolidated. To overcome this, it is necessary to import soil of a lighter nature as an overlay of at least 50cm in depth, having first dug and broken up the soil, or to insert drains. These can be ordinary field drain pipes, or made of baked clay or perforated plastic, which should be laid in a grid some 50–60cm below the surface, with a gentle fall to carry soakage away. The resulting water can be run into a ditch or a pool, or to moisture loving plants in another part of the garden. An alternative to drain pipes is to back-fill each narrow trench with shingle, broken stones, etc to a depth of 15–20cm. Having provided drainage, it is advisable also to add a light soil mix containing grit in some form as a growing medium, to a depth of at least 25cm. Soil mixtures are fully gone into later in the book.

Drainage is especially important if rocks are to be used where the basic soil is clay. The action of placing the rocks, and the weight of the rocks themselves, tends to ram or consolidate the soil, which in turn may impede natural water percolation.

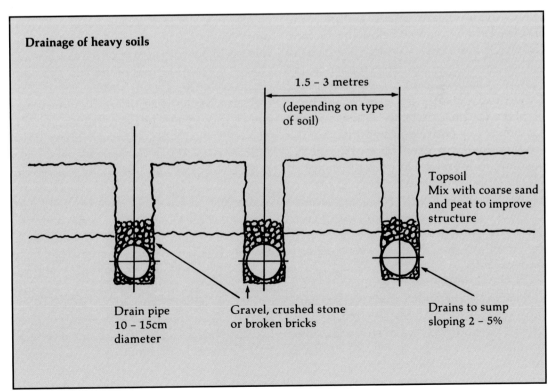

Drainage of heavy soils

1.5 – 3 metres

(depending on type of soil)

Topsoil
Mix with coarse sand and peat to improve structure

Drain pipe
10 – 15cm
diameter

Gravel, crushed stone
or broken bricks

Drains to sump
sloping 2 – 5%

Treatment of Weeds

It is of vital importance to eradicate pernicious weeds in all circumstances. Weeds such as couch grass, creeping thistle, bindweed, ground elder, mare's-tail and creeping sorrel, to mention some of the worst, must be killed at the outset. Forking out is not always effective and, although most weeds can be killed outright by chemicals, expert advice should always be taken as to which to use according to the type of weed, how and when it should be applied and how long the chemical will remain toxic in the soil. Annual weeds can also be a nuisance, but they are more easily dealt with by sprays or by hoeing; or, in the case of raised beds, by adding a sterilised soil mix to a sufficient depth above any natural soil, which nearly always holds seeds of annual weeds waiting to germinate.

Raised beds and terraces

A raised bed will appeal most to those with limited garden space. It is adaptable to any open situation and is to be recommended as an excellent way of showing alpines to their full advantage. Shape and size are a matter of personal choice; as are the extent to which it is raised above the natural garden level, and whether to make it an island site with all-round access or place it against an existing wall. In gardens where a narrow flower border against a wall has become more of a nuisance than an attraction, turning it into a raised bed is a good idea. But care should be taken if the flower border is against the wall of a house, as damp could penetrate into the house.

Although a raised bed can be of any height, generally a wall of about 60cm is quite adequate. The wall can be made of various materials. I do not recommend concrete because of its harsh appearance, but if it is used as a last resort it needs to be

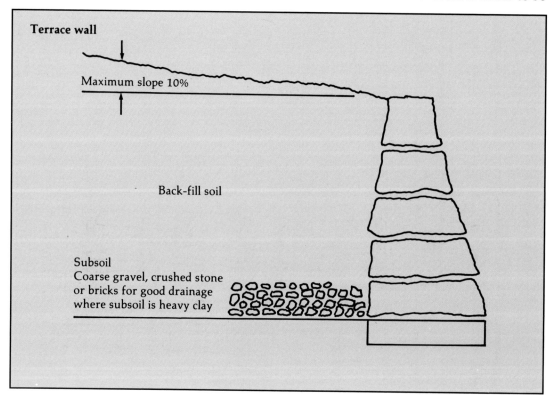

Terrace wall

Maximum slope 10%

Back-fill soil

Subsoil
Coarse gravel, crushed stone
or bricks for good drainage
where subsoil is heavy clay

toned down with a subdued colour cement coating. If the wall is to be built of bricks, it is better to use old ones as new bricks take some time to weather. But the best material is stone. The appearance is pleasing and it has the added advantage that niches can be left between stones, in which plants can grow by rooting through into the soil behind. Angular rocks or stones both look good and will fit in better with one another and makes cementing virtually unnecessary. Dry stone walling may be thought of as a craft, but with angular stones it is not beyond the capability of an amateur to build a sturdy wall. However, the earth beneath must be well consolidated to ensure stability.

It is vital to allow for drainage whether the wall is for terracing or for a raised bed. If no outlets are made when using cement to allow excess water to drain, the bed can become waterlogged. And this is especially important in the lower part of the wall. It is not so important if the wall is very low, or if the subsoil allows for adequate drainage.

One method of walling for a raised bed is to use dry stone walling with a backward slope. A slope of about 70–80 degrees adds strength against the pressure of the soil behind, and is necessary where the height of the bed, or of a terracing wall, is more than 60cm. In Munich Botanic Garden a raised bed was made with sloping walls about 1.5m high. It is an oblong, with all-round access and a flattish eye-level top of about 1.5m across; and the whole construction, including the sloping walls is designed to be fully clothed with plants. This particular design may not have a wide appeal, and watering could be a greater problem than drainage, but it is mentioned as an extreme example of a raised bed where the interest is centred on alpine plants in all their fascinating variety.

Within reasonable limits, the higher an island bed is raised, the greater the variety of plants that can be grown. And if it has a sunny side, it will also have a shady one

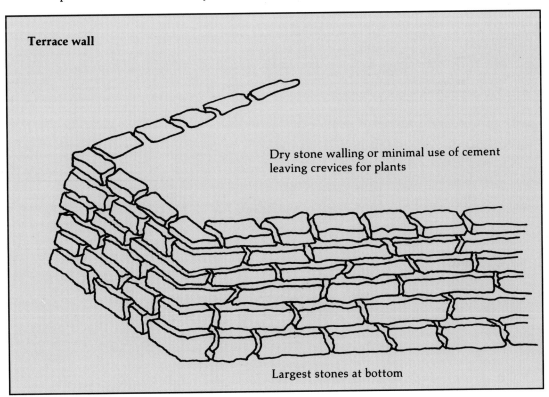

Terrace wall

Dry stone walling or minimal use of cement leaving crevices for plants

Largest stones at bottom

where shade-loving plants can be grown on a north-facing wall. But a high bed must not be so wide that it is necessary to climb up onto it for weeding or planting. And it is worth remembering that small rocks or stones are not as suitable as larger, angular ones for building a wall for high island beds, and the use of cement and whether to have a back slope would be a matter of discretion.

In recent years peat blocks have been recommended for use as a retaining wall for peat beds. In dry districts they are not very stable, as they tend to shrink and waste away, and they are not recommended for beds in open positions where mainly sun-loving, lime-tolerant plants are grown. There is a section covering peat beds further on in the book.

Advice on creating a terraced alpine bed is largely the same as that given for island, raised beds, or a one-sided border. Regardless of width, a two-sided border is in fact an island bed, and it can be very effective as a strip of no more than 50–60cm wide. If it is on a gentle slope, it can be levelled by a low

terrace wall on one side, the height of the wall depending on the angle of the slope. With most types of soil, slopes of more than 30 degrees are liable to erosion, and this can be prevented by levelling or reducing the slope to 10 degrees or less. If the slope is steep or continuous, then a series of terraces designed to grow plants both above the wall and in the cracks will give a spectacular display in spring and summer. In some countries complete hillsides are terraced for vines or other crops, but in a garden it would be necessary to have steps for access.

When terracing, care should be taken not only to build walls strong enough to withstand the pressure of the soil they retain, but also to conserve the topsoil. Topsoil is seldom deep on a natural slope, and it is a mistake to use subsoil for back-filling. Instead, the topsoil should be left virtually intact, except for being cleaned and loosened, and levelled off with imported soil.

Opposite: Sempervivum arachnoideum

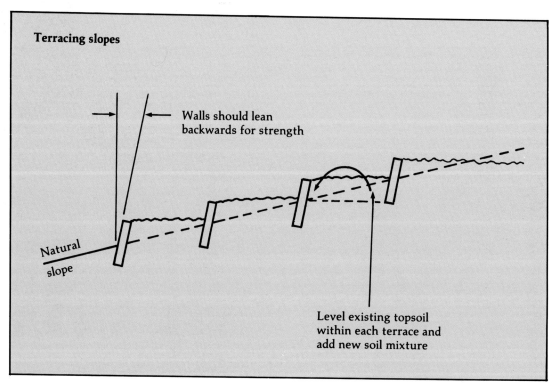

Terracing slopes

Walls should lean backwards for strength

Natural slope

Level existing topsoil within each terrace and add new soil mixture

'Walkabout' beds

A 'walkabout' bed is one which is on a more-or-less natural level, with stones, bricks or rocks as a kerb round the perimeter. As with a raised bed, it can be of any shape or size and, apart from the access stepping-stones, any stones used in the bed only serve to break up the flatness of the bed. But dwarf shrubs of many kinds, especially conifers, will serve to create focal points, thus making it a garden in miniature.

There are two advantages in raising a 'walkabout' bed a little. As soil needs to be added, this greatly reduces the growth of latent annual weeds and also can be of a type which is not already in the bed. So, one section of the bed could, for example, be filled with a peaty or lime-free soil for lime-hating plants. In order to be effective, the added soil should be at least 30cm deep.

Paving, crazy or otherwise, makes the best path round a 'walkabout' bed. The flat stones can be placed far enough apart to grow a selection of plants between them. The paving should be on a loose mixture so that the plant roots can take hold, but if the path is raised above garden or base level, it will also need a kerb to hold loose soil in around the edges.

Some people like to use rustic wood for the kerb of a 'walkabout' bed. The wood needs to be stripped of its bark to get rid of insect pests or slugs. Branches of durable hardwood, such as oak or elm, are best and should be between 15–30cm thick. If they are cut into lengths of two metres or more, they will hold the soil for several years. They should be laid singly round the out-side of the bed; if a second layer is needed, the branches should be wired or nailed together.

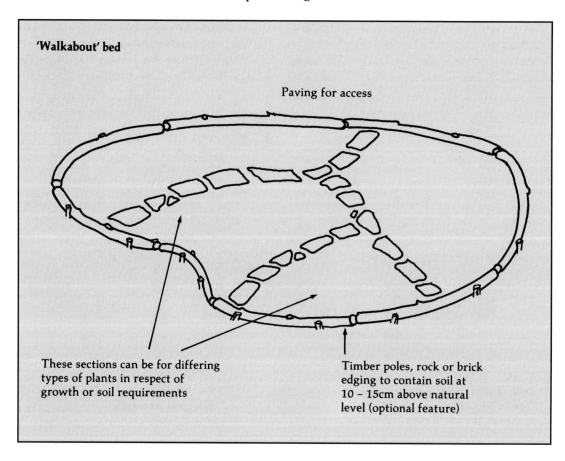

'Walkabout' bed

Paving for access

These sections can be for differing types of plants in respect of growth or soil requirements

Timber poles, rock or brick edging to contain soil at 10 – 15cm above natural level (optional feature)

Rock gardens

And finally, advice must be given for those who wish to build a rock garden, and who may see no incongruity in importing rocks to be placed far from their natural setting. But at least the rocks can appear as they would in nature and, if some elementary rules are followed, the effect can be very pleasing. The first is to avoid peaks and excessive height above the natural garden level. This is not only for obvious aesthetic reasons. A peak or miniature mountain would be prone to drying-out and, even if it became well established with plants, access would be difficult. It is much in keeping and effective to keep the contours low, depending on the size of the rock garden. The larger, the more imposing the rock formation can be, within reasonable limits and bearing in mind how expensive large rocks are.

Given a fairly open site well prepared for drainage and cleared of weeds, the best way to start is to make tiered outcrops. To some extent it is like terracing, using rocks as if they have always been there, protruding in layers from within a slope. The outcrops need be no more than 50cm high and at least half of each rock should be buried in the slope, holding in one ledge above and one at its foot to provide planting spaces. All the height required will be gained by a series of irregular ledges or outcrops and they should take up much less than half the whole space. Some rocks may be too heavy for one person to handle, unless the size is specified when they are ordered; but no matter what size the rocks are, the soil under them and round their bases should be well consolidated to ensure stability, by ramming with a piece of wood if necessary.

Sandstone or limestone rocks are best, but they are expensive and especially so if they have to be delivered from some distance. They are also heavy, and even a ten ton load will not make a large rock garden. This is another reason for using rocks sparingly as a means of enhancing the display of plants growing on different levels, rather than as a principal feature. As with walling, angular pieces of rock are

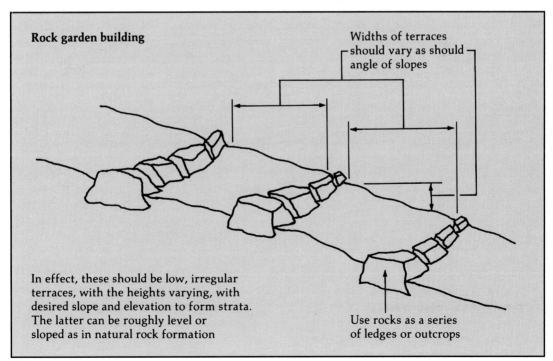

Rock garden building

Widths of terraces should vary as should angle of slopes

In effect, these should be low, irregular terraces, with the heights varying, with desired slope and elevation to form strata. The latter can be roughly level or sloped as in natural rock formation

Use rocks as a series of ledges or outcrops

best: they will fit more closely to form a ledge or outcrop, and will look much more natural than rounded boulders. Angular, oblong rocks should be placed with the thicker side down for stability and not stuck up on one end like huge teeth or gravestones.

If possible, a rock garden should be built into a slope. But if not, then it is best sited against a background of shrubs or evergreens, but not close enough for their roots to penetrate. A rock garden should never be placed near tree roots or overhanging branches either. And a low, island rock garden looks well in a flat garden, where the principal aim is to show the plants to their best advantage and the rocks are not prominent.

As with 'walkabout' beds, paving of some sort makes the best path in or beside a rock garden.

Soil mixtures and percolation

Almost invariably, additional soil will be needed for any of the constructions suggested. Buying soil from a reliable firm familiar with the type of soil in which alpines grow best, although initially expensive, may prove cheaper in the long run. But it is not difficult to make your own soil by mixing the three principal ingredients, of peat, gritty sand and loam. And of the three the most important is a weed-free, loamy soil. A good mixture is 50 per cent soil, with the balance made up of equal proportions of grit or sharp sand and peat. This should then be mixed with a fertiliser, preferably organic, containing both phosphates and potash, about half a kilogram to a cubic metre.

This additional soil should be used as a surface layer and, if sterilised, should remain weed-free for a year or two. Weeds will, of course, eventually appear even if the natural soil is deeply covered by sterilised soil. But, if annual weeds are not allowed to grow and seed again and perennial weeds dealt with on sight, then they should not be a problem.

The amount and type of grit which is added can vary depending on the nature of the soil, whether it is imported or already in the garden. If the soil is already stony or gravelly, then the proportion of grit can be reduced. But if the soil is heavy clay or generally has a low content of sand and stone, then it needs the addition of both small grit and sharp sand. Without the grit, a clay soil tends to pan down when wet, even with the addition of fine sand. And this leads to poor drainage when wet, and hardness when dry. As both inhibit good root systems, it is harder for the plants to survive in winter. Most plants native to high altitudes, or where snow persists well into spring, grow in stony soil. And this is important as in spring the melting snow sinks in and the soil below does not become dry again until fading and seeding take place. For this reason, for alpines grown at low altitudes, winter drainage is the most vital factor.

Providing additional moisture during dry summers is simple in free-draining soil. But with heavy or clay soils (those which can be balled-up in the hand when damp), it is necessary to add some porous material. The best are crushed rock, bricks or even clinker ash, with flinty gravel a poor fourth. If lime-hating plants are to be grown, the possible lime content of these materials must be borne in mind. To test the porosity of the soil is quite simple. Make a little heap of three of four shovelsful, then pat the top to make it slightly dished. Pour some water gently on to the dished top and, if the water runs through into the soil rather than forming a puddle or running off, then the mixture is right. Another easy test before making up the porous mixture is to try balling up a handful of the damp, basic soil. If it crumbles easily or does not consolidate, then there is no need to add the porous materials.

Different types of soil mixture

Soil mixtures can, of course, be varied according to the type of plants which are to be grown. In a garden with more than 6.5 lime content (this figure is roughly neutral), a section can be made suitable for lime-hating plants. Lime-free soil, or a peat bed, to a depth of 30–35cm can quite easily be achieved. Another section can be made suitable for scree plants, most of which are lime-tolerant, by mixing half the soil with rock chippings, broken bricks, etc to a similar depth. A scree bed should be well elevated and, to reduce the risk of its scorching or drying out, you can spread fine stone chippings to a depth of 3–4cm over the whole area after planting. Very small gravel, known as pea-shingle, will serve the same purpose and can be used wherever alpines are grown. It helps to prevent annual weeds from seeding, and keeps the soil better aerated because on some soils rain or water leaves a harmful crust on the surface as it dries.

Some alpines prefer poor to rich soil – stony rather than one containing humus. It is surprising to see them growing in the wild with their roots getting all they need by foraging in the crevices of a rock face. Others are happy in what appears to be sand or rock rubble, the make-up of scree being the debris of eroded cliffs or outcrops. This can be imitated in gardens quite satisfactorily with broken stone, brick, sandy gravel and clinker ash, which feels quite sharp when you squeeze it. Plants like the varied and interesting houseleeks (*Sempervivum*) and several silver-leaved carpeters grow best in these arid mixtures, as they need very little water.

Peat beds

More needs to be said about peat beds which, because they are an easy, inexpensive way of growing a wide variety of plants, are becoming increasingly popular. It is advisable to use specially cut turves for walling. These are larger than ordinary building bricks and will make a more durable wall than turves cut for fuel. The turves should also contain heather or other roots, which hold the peat together for a year or two. Such blocks are taken from the upper layers in a natural peat bed. If the blocks are on the small side, or have a tendency to break up when being handled, then the walls should be built with two widths of turves, placed with overlapping joints as in conventional brickwork. If a wall higher than two layers of turf blocks is needed, place every third, fourth or fifth block at right angles, bedding it in to the back-fill of loose peat mixture. Where the wall is to be higher than 40–50cm, provide a little back slope to the wall as well.

An even better way of gaining height is to terrace with peat blocks, leaving planting space at the foot of each. This gives a more informal appearance than building a higher single wall with a level bed on top.

Peat beds should never be placed in full sun. Not only because so many peat-loving plants like some shade, but also because as peat holds up to eight times its own weight in water when soaked, if it is allowed to dry out it becomes sterile. And when peat becomes really dry, water will run off it at first instead of soaking in.

The best situation for a peat bed is on the north side of a house or wall, or wherever trees can give it some shade without their roots penetrating the bed or their branches dripping on to it.

To reduce the fluffiness in peat, you should add only sand and fertiliser or a little soil. And because it is so light in texture, the planting should be level, or nearly so. An annual top dressing of fertilised peat mixture in spring or autumn is advisable to repair natural shrinkage and wastage.

Pulverised bark or leaf mould can be used as an alternative to peat, but these are not so good and are not so easy to obtain.

Other uses for alpines

Many dwarf, hardy perennials, usually considered to be purely alpine or rock garden plants, are very suitable for growing in front of taller subjects. Many gardens have a border of perennials, either the conventional one-sided type with a backing or the more modern and effective, less troublesome island bed. The former should be planned with the tallest plants at the back, and the latter with the tallest in the centre. Heights can then be graded down to the most dwarf at the front and it is there that a variety of alpines can look most effective, adding greatly to the diversity and interest of the bed.

Naturally a selection for frontal border groups should exclude the low, carpeting or trailing alpines as well as the slow growing, hummock forming ones. But there are many in the range which are mainly erect growing to about 15–20cm high, which are fully adaptable. They include free growing, selected kinds of *Achillea, Armeria, Aster, Campanula, Dianthus, Geranium, Helianthemum, Iris, Potentilla* and some primulas, *Ranunculus, Scabiosa, Sedum, Sisyrinchium, Veronica* and *Viola*. It is more effective to place the slow growing kinds in groups, with the taller ones behind.

Path edging

Some alpines have real value as edging plants beside a path, especially if the path is made of gravel or paving. This edging can be of either all one kind, or made up of a variety of alpines. Evergreen alpines look effective all the year round, and are trouble free. Outstanding of these are *Armeria maritima* in variety, *Campanula muralis, Dianthus*, the primrose varieties of *Primula, Scabiosa graminifolia, Achillea tomentosa* and violas. They would need no attention for several years, and then only replanting to reduce their spread, and all are worthwhile both for flower and foliage. For a shady walk, *Epimedium* would do well.

Where used as an edging to grass paths, difficulty when mowing and possible competition from overhang should be considered. It can help to have some bricks or stones between the path and the plants.

Opposite: Campanula portenschlagiana

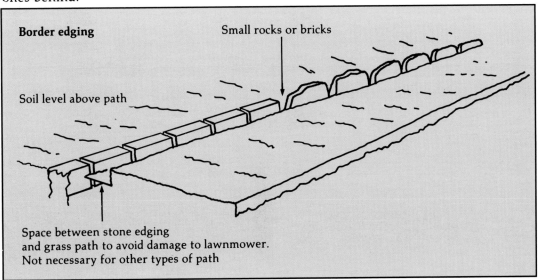

Border edging

Small rocks or bricks

Soil level above path

Space between stone edging and grass path to avoid damage to lawnmower. Not necessary for other types of path

A garden in a trough

Two other means of growing alpines may appeal, especially to those who have virtually no garden space, or where gardening is not possible. The first is to grow alpines in a trough. One or more troughs take up very little space on a patio for example, and are very suitable for growing a wide variety of choicer, slow growing plants. Real antique, stone troughs are expensive, but there are modern, cheaper substitutes in which plants will grow just as well.

A trough should not be less than 15cm deep inside, ideally 20–25cm or more, and must have a drainage point. If there is only one hole at the end, tilt the trough slightly towards it, whether the trough is at ground level or raised. Before planting slow growing alpines in the trough, a layer of broken bricks should be placed in the bottom, topped with a gritty mixture of soil, as for scree. And a 1–2cm covering of stone chippings after planting is advisable. If you want to break up the flat surface you can place one or two stones in the trough, or plant a slow growing, dwarf conifer, such as *Juniperus communis* 'Compressa'. A space of about 12cm should be left between the plants for the very close growing, and the effect of the trough is greatly enhanced by planting alpines which will trail or hang above the rim.

Alpine house

A glass alpine house is the other means of growing a collection of choice subjects, especially those allergic to wet winters. It can be any size, unheated, but with ample ventilation which should be left open except during very severe or stormy spells. The shelf should be at a convenient height and made of durable material which can take fine shingle on which to stand the plants in pots or pans. Some alpine enthusiasts construct a miniature rock garden on the

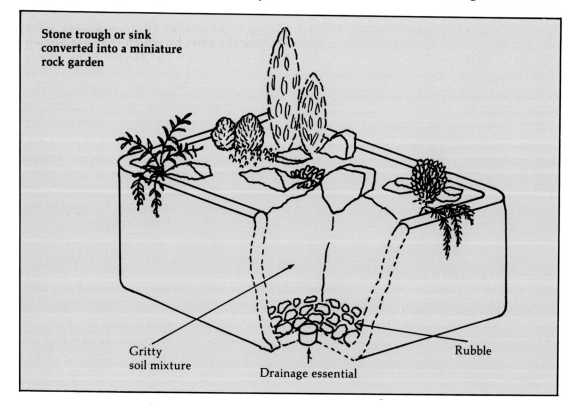

Stone trough or sink converted into a miniature rock garden

Gritty soil mixture

Drainage essential

Rubble

shelf, using tufa rock as it is light and the roots of the plants can penetrate its porous structure. The roof needs to have some shading in the summer, the best being blinds made of split cane or thin plastic strips, which can be rolled up in winter.

Although an alpine house is a specialist means of growing alpines, often attracting the connoisseur, there is no reason why anyone who loves alpines should not invest in an alpine house. It is free from the vagaries of the weather, and can give a great deal of pleasure.

How to choose and plant alpines

Having already emphasised the importance of choosing a site, taking suitability into account, some advice on making a selection of plants will be helpful. When making their selection, some readers may find plant names unnecessarily formidable. The first thing is to accept that all plants have botanical names by which they are known internationally. To depart from these names, and to give the plants common or folk names, would result in confusion. The genus, or generic name always comes first, and a folk name often applies only to one of many species in a genus. For example, take *Campanula*, which covers the folk name of harebell and bellflower. The specific name comes next and, if one has the true harebell, it is *Campanula rotundifolia*, but there are hundreds of other species which have no folk name and this is where it could become confusing. A cultivar is a form, variety or clone of garden origin, and takes third place; and so a white form of harebell in cultivation is *Campanula rotundifolia* 'Spetchley White'. Both Latin and Greek are used in plant names, and the specific name often describes some distinguishing feature.

Above: Sempervivums in trough

Campanula refers to the bell-like flower (as in campanology), whilst *rotundifolia* refers to the rounded (rotund) leaves. Plant names become very interesting once their necessity for identification is understood.

The most important thing is to choose plants best suited for a given site. Success in growing plants depends on the suitability of the soil, climate, etc as described in the list of general recommendations. Many are widely adaptable, but vigorous plants can smother choicer, slow growing plants if they are planted too close to each other. A few are so invasive that they should be avoided altogether: and, for this reason, it can be risky to acquire plants, or accept them as gifts, without knowing their growing habits.

The very best way to make a selection of plants is from a specialist's catalogue, or from noting the names of those seen in other gardens. In most gardens the plants are established and can be fully appreciated, which is not the case in hastily planted exhibits at flower shows. And, although there is seldom a wide variety on offer in garden centres, at least the plants can be seen in flower and taken away for immediate planting.

There is no hard and fast rule for the best time to plant alpines. If the selected plant is pot grown, then it can be planted at virtually any time except when it is very wet or frosty. Generally speaking, the best times for planting are spring and early autumn, but much depends on the site being well prepared. Perfect conditions are more critical for smaller bare-rooted cuttings and seedlings. And choice or slow growing plants, not grown in pots, may not survive a dry summer if planted in spring or a harsh winter if planted in autumn. Planting is very simple; make a hole with a trowel, remove the plant from the pot and insert in to the hole. Always make sure that plants are well watered before planting and, if the soil is very dry, fill each hole with water with the plant in position before filling and firming in the soil.

When first embarking on alpines, most people will prefer to have one of a kind for variety, and in small beds or rock gardens this is preferable. In larger areas, groups of not less than three of a kind will give a more spectacular display. And, for interest's sake, plants should be labelled. At first, names may seem unimportant but those who know the names of their alpine plants get the greatest pleasure from them. To know them is to love them, and loving plants is a very precious gift and a wonderful antidote to the pressures of modern life.

It is not necessary for amateurs to propogate alpines. But some people may want to raise some from seed as it it cheaper than buying flowering-sized plants. Raising plants from seed can be difficult: some will breed true, others will come in a mixture of colours, including the popular *Aubrieta*, some *Dianthus* and *Helianthemum*. And seed may be difficult to obtain, or may take a long time to germinate and need special care. Generally, it is more satisfactory to plant a rock garden with plants rather than attempt to raise them from seed. And, in the long run, may be more economical. However, it is great fun to raise seed occasionally, and also take cuttings. The descriptive list gives the best method of increase for most kinds.

AN ALPHABETICAL LIST

The following symbols indicate preferred sites:

- ☼ sunny

- ◐ partly shaded

- ● fully shaded

ACAENA ☼

Rosaceae

Vigorous carpeting plants, which will grow in almost any soil and give good foliage cover. *A. buchananii* makes a dense mat of soft, pea-green foliage. *A. inermis*, of similiar habit, is bluish-bronze and *pulchella* reddish-purple. All the above are better as paving plants, for the flowers are insignificant.

A. microphylla is outstanding for its russet-brown mats and bright red, burr-like flowers which bloom for many weeks in late summer. *A. adscendens* grows taller, to 15cm, with arching stems carrying grey-green leaves and reddish burrs – good as ground cover; whilst 'Blue Haze' will inhabit a wall.

Acaenas can also be used as summer cover for spring flowering bulbs – and all are easy to increase by division of well established plants in spring.

ACHILLEA ☼

Compositae

These give good foliage cover and a show of yellow or white flowers on flattish heads in summer. *A. argentea* has tufty silver foliage 10cm high, with heads of white flowers at 15cm. *A. aurea* and *chrysocoma* are much alike with a vigorous spread of soft, light greenery, topped with bright yellow heads to 20cm. *A. tomentosa* is closer growing with darker greenery and deeper yellow flowers at 20cm, from June to August. *A.* 'King Edward' has very pleasing primrose-yellow flowers for most of the summer.

All the above need very good drainage, but are easy to increase by division of well established plants in spring or early autumn. Achilleas are effective with campanulas.

ADONIS ◖

Ranunculaceae

These are choice, slow growing plants, with the one fault of some having a long dormant period. They need good but well-drained soil, and take well to peat beds.

A. amurensis 'Plena' flowers from February to April, 15cm tall, with fine double, greenish-yellow flowers and is increased by division in early autumn when the clumpy plant is large enough. Although *A. vernalis* is slower to increase, it has charming yellow flowers on ferny-leaved bush growth, from March to May, 30–35cm tall where happy. *A. volgensis* is similar, but flowers a week or two earlier.

Provided the adonis are not smothered, ajugas are attractive in association.

Left: Acaena microphylla

AETHIONEMA ☼

Cruciferae

These sun-lovers are best in poor or stony soil, and are excellent wall plants. *A. grandiflorum* and *A. pulchellum* are much alike with a low twiggy habit, bluish foliage to 25cm and smothered in rounded spikes of clear, light pink flowers in early summer. They may be raised from seed, but the cultivars 'Warley Rose' and the slightly deeper pink 'Warley Ruber' can only be increased from summer cuttings under glass. Both have intense pink flowers above the blue-grey foliage on compact 15cm bushy growth.

Above: Aethionema 'Warley Rose'
Left: Adonis amurensis 'Plena'

AJUGA ◑

Labiatae

These make attractive leafy mats of real value when not too dry, and have short flower spikes in spring and early summer. They form rosettes of shiny leaves, rooting as they spread, making for rapid increase. Useful under deciduous shrubs and pleasant in association with silver or gold foliage.

A. reptans has several cultivars, including white and pink-flowered, as distinct from the basic blue type. 'Burgundy Glow' has crinkled, shiny foliage variegated pink, bronze and cream, with A. reptans 'Multicolor' ('Rainbow') having several shades. Both have blue spikes in spring. 'Pink Elf' is a dwarf form, and A. reptans 'Variegata' spreads quickly by runners, with creamy-marked leaves. A. metallica has dense, shiny, crinkled leaves of deepest blue and A. pyramidalis is best for flowering, with spikes of gentian blue to 20cm, but needs a damp soil.

Increased by division of well established plants in spring or early autumn.

Below: Allium beesianum

ALLIUM ☼

Liliaceae

Only the smallest non-invasive species can be recommended as members of the bulbous onion family. All have heads, sometimes dangling, of small, brightly-coloured flowers. Some have a long period of dormacy, but all are readily increased by division when dormant.

A. cyaneum and A. beesianum are both excellent for their sheaves of blue flowers on 12cm stems. A. oreophilium ostrowskianum has tufts of narrow leaves with umbels of broad, carmine-red flowers. A. moly, a yellow species, should be avoided, being invasive, but A. cyathophorum 'Farreri' is recommended for its heads of purple flowers, 15cm tall. A. narcissiflorum is only 10cm with nodding bells of wine red, whilst A. pulchellum has quite large heads of deep pink, 15cm tall.

All these alliums are summer flowering, and are best combined with plants of a mounded or cushion habit, such as the dwarf dianthus.

Opposite: Androsace languinosa

ALYSSUM ☼

Cruciferae

A. saxatile and its variations are showy and deservedly popular for spring display. They form robust mounded-to-spreading growth above ground from a single non-spreading root system, with sprays of small flowers in yellow shades covering the grey foliage. The yellow species are easily raised from seed, but variations come from framed cuttings in late summer or autumn. *A. saxatile* is offered in *A.s.* 'Compactum', but is not really compact when old, whereas the cultivar 'Gold Ball' is. Both of these are bright yellow. *A. s.* 'Citrinum' is a lemon yellow, and 'Dudley Neville' a primrose yellow. The double-flowered *A.s.* 'Plenum' is very showy with fuller flowers, but is less vigorous.

All the above need sun, like lime and good drainage, and are increased by seed.

ANACYCLUS ☼

Compositae

A. depressus is not long-lived and needs sharp drainage or scree soil. It forms flat rosettes of finely cut leaves producing large, white, daisy flowers which are crimson underneath. Only about 8cm high, and flowering in summer, it can be increased by seed.

ANDROSACE ☼

Primulaceae

These plants are widely distributed in nature. Most of them form hummocks of rosettes, some grey-green, and are easy in very well-drained soil. Rounded heads of mostly pink flowers come in early summer. *A. sarmentosa (primuloides)* is the best-known of this type, growing 5–10cm tall, with the cultivar 'Watkinsii' having rosy-red flowers. *A. sempervivoides* is also attractive. *A. villosa* and *A. microphylla* are smaller and both are safest in scree conditions. *A. lanuginosa* and its cultivars are distinct with their silvery, trailing stems carrying heads of pink or near-white flowers in later summer. These are good subjects for a sunny wall.

Androsaces are best increased from cuttings, but the rosette-forming kinds will divide with care if pieces are detached with sufficient root for them to survive.

ANDRYALA ☼

Compositae

A. aghardii needs a warm place and very good drainage to show off its silvery tufts of foliage set with vivid yellow flowers for several weeks of summer. It grows to 15–20cm, and can be increased from late summer cuttings or seed.

ANEMONE

Ranunculaceae

These differ widely in origin and cultural need and are for sun or partial shade. *A. baicalensis* has large white flowers on 20cm stems, and *A. magellanica*, of similar height, has cream flowers. *A. palmata* at 12cm is a choice, white-flowered species needing full sun, and though the near-red *A. x lesseri* is tall at 30cm it is a splendid plant. All the above flower in early summer, and can be increased by division when large enough.

A. nemorosa is the wood anemone, easy to grow and naturalise. The roots, like tiny brown sticks, are difficult to find in a bed and plants should be sited where they can remain. The species with white or pale blue flowers are best confined to a shady corner, or grown in grass like snowdrops. *A. n. robinsoniana* is a fine blue, and *A. n.* 'Alba Plena' is an outstanding double white. All grow to 10–12cm and prefer heavy to very light soil. *A. ranunculoides* is of similar growth with bright yellow flowers. All have a long dormant period, and can be overplanted with the small ajugas, but should not be grown amongst choicer alpines. See also *Pulsatilla*.

ANTENNARIA ☼

Compositae

These are easily-grown carpeters, rooting as they spread with short, tufty, greyish leaves. Flowers are on little clusters in early summer. Useful for paving or as cover for alpine bulbs, which will grow through the carpet of the smaller growing types.

A. aprica is vigorous with greyish foliage and white flowers to 15cm. A. dioica is seen in white, pale pink and rosy-red variants, all 10cm; but A. d. 'Minima' is a distinctive pink dwarf. All are easily divided in spring or early autumn, and look well beneath dwarf shrubs and conifers.

Opposite: Anemone x lesseri
Below: Anthemis rudolphiana

ANTHEMIS ☼

Compositae

These are easy in any well-drained soil, but white-flowered A. cupaniana, though showy and long flowering, spreads too quickly for small beds. It has finely divided leaves, as has the less rampant A. triumfettii. A. pedunculata 'Tuberculata', also white-flowered to 20cm, is grey-leaved with clumpy growth. The most valuable as an alpine plant is the silvery-leaved A. rudolphiana (A. biebersteiniana) with deep golden flowers. These are borne erectly to 15cm and make a fine show in early summer. All the above can be divided or raised from seed.

A. nobilis is the herb camomile with aromatic, deep green foliage. It grows close to the surface with a fairly rapid spread; and though the double white-flowered A. n. 'Plena' is of limited value as a garden plant, only 10cm tall, the non-flowering A. n. 'Treneague' is used for lawns or a walk-upon carpeter.

ANTHYLLIS ☼

Leguminosae

Long-lived, sub-shrubby plant of value in well-drained sunny places, including walls. *A. hermanniae* makes a dense, twiggy mound of greyish hue, with an abundance of small yellow, pea-shaped flowers in summer, 20cm high. *A. montana* is best in the deep pink-to-red *A.m.* 'Rubra'. It makes a surface spread of silvery leaves covered with clover-like heads in early summer to make a bright display, 8cm high.

Seed increase is possible, as is careful division of established plants in spring.

Below: Anthyllis montana 'Rubra'
Below right: Aquilegia discolor
Opposite top: Arabis 'Corfe Castle'
Opposite bottom: Arenaria montana

AQUILEGIA ◑

Ranunculaceae

The columbines have a wide range in nature. Some of the most dwarf are best in scree soil, other prefer some damp and shade, but unfortunately few are long-lived. These include *A. bertolonii* with large blue flowers on 12cm stems, and *A. discolor*, blue and white at only 8cm. *A. scopulorum* has soft blue flowers and silvery foliage, 12cm. These three are best in scree or rock crevices. *A. flabellata* 'Nana', available in both blue and white, 20cm, is very robust as is the charming blue and white *glandulosa*. These both like a cool position with peaty soil.

Aquilegia can only be increased from seed, and this does not invariably produce plants true to name, except in the most dwarf kinds. All flower in early summer, and seed should be sown outdoors when ripe.

ARABIS ☼

Cruciferae

Spring flowering plants with much the same general habit as *Aubrieta*. *A. albida* and its double form, both white, although useful for banks or edgings, are too rampant for small sites. A cultivar named 'Rosabella' is more compact with pink flowers to 10cm. The hybrid 'Corfe Castle' has rosy-red flowers above a leafy evergreen mat in spring, to make it the most colourful of all.

Well-drained soil is essential for these and the rather short-lived species. These make low hummocks, which are dividable, or increased from cuttings in autumn. *A. ferdinandi-coburgii* 'Variegata' is tiny with white flowers above a mat of variegated foliage, through which such early flowering bulbs as chionodoxa will grow, its blue contrasting effectively. At 8cm it roots as it spreads and is useful between rocks.

ARENARIA ☼

Caryophyllaceae

Easy, close growing plants for early summer, nearly all white flowered. *A. balearica* is the only exception to a general preference for sun. It grows as a mere film of bright green, dotted with white flowers only 5cm high. It needs a dampish, half-shady place, is quick to spread, but it is not hardy in very cold districts. *A. caespitosa* 'Aurea' is similar, but needs sun; it has permanently golden foliage and sparse white flowers, and needs to be frequently divided and replanted to retain colour and compactness.

A. ledebouriana has close, grassy foliage and small white flowers, but the brightest is *A. montana*, whose somewhat trailing, deep

green foliage is smothered in larger, pure white flowers in summer. Both are about 10cm. *A. pinifolia* is also attractive, with a mounded, narrow-leaved growth.

A. nevadensis and *A. tetraquetra* make curiously attractive cushions, but are best in scree conditions. Both rank as collectors' items.

ARISARUM ◑ ●

Araceae

A. proboscideum makes a low mass of arrow-shaped leaves in a cool, shady spot, through which appear what look like mouse tails in early summer. A curiosity which dies back to dormancy from September to March. Increased by division of well established plants in spring or autumn.

ARMERIA ☼

Plumbaginaceae

Often called thrift, these are first-rate alpines, giving excellent evergreen ground cover like tufted grass, and a show of flowers on rounded heads in early summer. The choicest and slowest to grow, as low mounds, is *A. caespitosa*: it is for well-drained soil or scree, with clear pink flowers only 5cm tall. *A. maritima* is a variable, easily grown species. The brightest and nearest to red is 'Dusseldorf Pride', 15–20cm; 'Vindictive' is pink; and 'Alba' pure white, 12–15cm, flowering in early summer. *A corsica* is distinctive for its heads of a brick-red colour on 25cm stems.

All are easy to divide in spring or autumn, except *A. caespitosa* which is best from seed or base cuttings.

Below: Armeria caespitosa

ARNEBIA ☼

Boraginaceae

A. echioides forms fleshy-rooted plants with hairy green leaves, and in late spring sends up clusters of bright yellow flowers on which are maroon spots. It is called the Prophet's Flower because it is said that the Prophet stumbled while walking on stony ground, and as he fell he left the imprint of his hand in the five maroon spots on each flower.

Though not difficult in well-drained light soil, this remains a rare and choice plant, about 25cm high; it can be divided in autumn, with care. It contrasts well with pulsatillas and *Phlox canadensis*.

ARTEMISIA ☼

Compositae

The only species recommended as an alpine is *A. schmidtiana* 'Nana' for a very well-drained position. It forms a low mound of bright silvery, filigree foliage, making a good backcloth to other plants with colourful flowers. Its own flowers are greyish and of no importance.

Increased by division in spring, or from summer cuttings.

ASARINA ◑

Scrophulariaceae

A. procumbens (formerly *Antirrhinum asarina*). This resents being sun-baked, but in a cool place it spreads between rocks or walls to give a long succession of creamy-coloured, snapdragon-like flowers, 10cm. Division in spring.

Below: Artemisia schmidtiana 'Nana'

ASPERULA ☼

Rubiaceae

Includes some choice diminutive species. *A. capitata* is easy to grow, forming slow-spreading hummocks with tiny, shell-pink flowers in early summer, 5cm. *A. lilaciflora caespitosa* makes a prostrate, deep green mat, set with clear pink flowers for many weeks, only 3cm. *A. nitida* makes a dense green cushion studded with pink flowers, 8cm.

A. suberosa is a treasure, having more upright, grey-leaved stems to 6cm, with clusters of clear pink, tubular flowers in late spring. Both are best in scree-type soil and resent winter wet.

Careful division in early spring.

ASPLENIUM ◑

Polypodiaceae

Two species of evergreen, rosette-forming ferns suitable for shady nooks and crevices. One is the dainty, grey-leaved *A. rutamuraria* with deeply-cut, rosette leaves; the other is *A. trichomanes* with fingered, bright green fronds.

Increased by division of well established plants in spring or autumn.

Below: Asperula suberosa

ASTER ☼

Compositae

The few dwarf species of this genus, which includes michaelmas daisy, are worth considering. They are not all well known, but they deserve to be.

A. alpinus makes a neat, easily divided clump, having wide, yellow-centred daisy flowers in spring and early summer. It is very variable, with white, pink-lilac and blue shades available to name; height 15–20cm. *A. natalensis* creeps to form mats of deep green rosettes, with bright blue flowers for many weeks, on 20cm stems. *A. sativus atrocaeruleus* has smaller, clear blue flowers from compact leafy plants, 15cm, for much of the summer. *A. spectabilis* is autumn flowering from mats of leathery leaves with sprays of intense blue, 20cm.

All these are fairly adaptable and easy from division. They are best in company with yellow-flowered subjects.

Above: Aster sativus astrocaeruleus
Overleaf: Astilbe simplicifolia 'Sprite'

ASTILBE ◑

Saxifragaceae

Without exception, these like moist, humus-rich soil and some shade in return for a bright show of flowers between June and September. All have very attractive summer foliage even when not in flower and, though old plants divide readily, any obsolete woody root should be discarded when replanting.

A. crispa has dark green, crinkly foliage in dense mound formation, above which come 12cm pokery spikes of bright pink in the best cultivar 'Perkeo'. *A. chinensis* 'Pumila' is very vigorous with lots of lilac-pink spikes in late summer, 20–25cm. *A. glaberrima* 'Saxosa' is the smallest at only 8cm tall; a perfect miniature, but demanding cooler conditions, preferring peaty soil. *A. simplicifolia* has a dwarf pink form 'Nana', only 12cm tall, and has produced a splendid hybrid named 'Sprite'. This makes deep green, lacy foliage and gives a profusion of delicate, shell-pink flowers on 20–25cm spikes, and has been plant of the year in both the USA and Germany.

AUBRIETA ☼

Cruciferae

Amongst the most popular of plants, these make a brilliant display in spring from March to June. They will come from seed, but not true to colour. There is no excuse for retaining some of the older, paler shades with inferior flowers, when modern varieties are available, either from seed or plants, to name and colour. All they need is good drainage: they prefer soil to peat and are partial to lime. As soon as flowering is over, plants should be trimmed with shears. They will increase by division or cuttings in autumn. Named varieties offer ample choice of colour, and A. 'Bressingham Pink' is an attractive semi-double with clear bright pink flowers, and A. 'Bressingham Red' a single with clear red flowers.

Below: Aubreita 'Bressingham Red'

BLECHNUM ◑

Polypodiaceae

B. *penna-marina* is another diminutive creeping fern with bronzy-green, leathery fronds, for crevices or shaded walls. B. *spicant* is larger with deeply divided centre fronds to 30cm above a green rosette formation. Both are evergreen, and B. *spicant* will grow in sun where not too dry.

Division of all ferns is best in spring and summer.

BOLAX ☼

Hydrocotylaceae

B. *glabaria* (*Azorella trifurcata*) is grown for its bright green, rosetted cushions, which steadily expand. They bear tiny yellow flowers. An easy plant for any well-drained soil, it will respond to division in early autumn or spring.

BRACHYCOME ☼

Compositae

B. *rigidula* makes a 12cm dark green mound, carrying lavender-blue, daisy flowers for many weeks. Comes from seed or will divide.

BULBINELLA ☼

Liliaceae

B. *hookeri* is a choice, distinctive, semi-bulbous plant from New Zealand, with bronzy-green, narrow leaves. In early summer come stems of bright yellow, pokery spikes to 30cm. Increase by seed or division.

CALAMINTHA ☼ ◐

Labiatae

C. nepetoides is fairly tall at 30–35cm, but makes a fine display of soft lavender-blue flowers for many weeks in late summer, in sun or partial shade. It is a trouble-free plant with many uses, such as topping a wall or in front of perennials with a good upright habit. Divide in spring.

CALTHA ☼

Ranunculaceae

As kingcup or marsh marigold, *C. palustris* is often seen and admired in the wild, but the more compact *C. p.* 'Plena' is a very good garden plant. So long as its soil does not dry out in summer, it will give no trouble, and provide a bright display of fully double, deep yellow flowers on semi-prostrate sprays above its rounded leaves in April and May, height 15–20cm. Also seen in a single white form. But the best white species is *C. leptosepala*, with pure white sprays of open flowers on erect 12cm stems in spring.

Both can easily be divided after flowering and combine admirably with cardamines.

CAMPANULA ☼ ◐

Campanulaceae

A large and varied genus of great value, for most of them flower after the spring flush of alpines is over. Some species are very choice or difficult, others are short-lived and a few are weedy. The list below are all worthwhile recommending as having reli-

ability and merit, and include good cultivars such as 'Birch Hybrid'. This flowers on and off for much of the year, forming neat clumpy plants with deep lavender-blue upturned flowers to 15cm.

C. carpatica is best in its named varieties, which all flower in the period from June to August, with mainly upturned, cup or saucer-shaped flowers above bushy summer growth. 'Blue Moonlight' is china blue at 15cm. 'Chewton Joy' has a profusion of smaller, light blue flowers only 10cm tall; 'Hannah', of similar habit, is pure white and 'Isobel' deep blue at 20cm.

C. 'Constellation' and 'Stella' are both hybrids of compact mounded habit with outspreading sprays of lavender-blue flowers which last many weeks. *C. garganica* is of similar habit, but more tightly mounded; and there are taller variations as well as the choicer, deep lavender-blue flowered 'W H Paine'. An outstanding hybrid of *C. garganica* is 'Dickson's Gold' with bright gold foliage and starry blue flowers. These are good wall plants.

Campanulas with a creeping habit, which die back in winter, include the dainty blue *cochlearifolia*, the white 'Hallii' and larger, deep blue 'Oakington', all 6–8cm. 'G F Wilson' also runs below ground and carries large violet-blue flowers 8–10cm; with *pulla* dangling purple-blue bells to 6cm, and *pulloides* like a larger version of it at 12cm. These types wander somewhat and may need curbing.

Not so with *C. portenschlagiana* (*C. muralis*), which has clumpy growth and lavender-blue flowers about 12cm, and is useful in walls in sun or shade.

C. carpatica turbinata and its cultivars grow more like dwarf *carpitaca* types in shades of blue and violet. 'Molly Pinsent', 'Stansfieldii' and 'Norman Grove' are hybrids with clumpy growth, not evergreen, making a mounded display in varying shades of lavender-blue in July and August, 10–20cm. All the above are virtually trouble-free in any well-drained soil, limy or acid.

The true harebell *C. rotundifolia* does not take well to cultivation, though there are easier variations in deep blue and white in 'Covadonga' and 'Spetchley White'. One species to avoid for being weedy is *C. poscharskyana*. *C. wockei* is a choice species of tiny, bushy habit, darkly foliaged with small, deep blue open bells, but the cross I made which produced 'Puck' is a distinctive improvement which always appeals.

Campanulas can be divided in spring, and *C. carpatica* germinates well from seed, in mixture. All associate happily with dwarf shrubs and sedums, yellow or pink.

Right: Campanula carpatica 'Blue Moonlight'
Below: Campanula portenschlagiana

CARDAMINE ☼

Cruciferae

All these like moisture, whether in sun or part shade. They also respond to being divided and replanted every two years, after flowering, and will then give a bright display in spring. The single flowered *C. pratensis*, known as the cuckoo flower, is often seen wild, but its double form 'Plena' is very attractive with erect stems carrying lilac-mauve flowers, 20cm. A more vigorous species, with fairly rapid surface spread, is *C. latifolia* which makes a splendid show of pale violet flowers on 30cm stems. Both are excellent with calthas.

CARDUNCELLUS ☼

Compositae

C. rhaponticoides is quite outstanding with its evergreen rosette of leathery leaves close to the soil, up to 20cm across. In early summer comes a large, rounded, stemless head, like a ball of lilac-blue. The plant is easy in well-drained soil, and it can be increased with cuttings from its fleshy roots.

CAREX ☼ ◑

Cyperaceae

This is sedge, and as a genus has little to commend it for garden cultivation. As a species *C. morrowii* is useful evergreen ground cover, but the cultivar 'Evergold' (*C. morrowii* 'Aurea Variegata') is outstandingly valuable. The bladed leaves, of bright golden-yellow with a thin green line, arch over to cover 30cm or more across as a

shapely mound, effective throughout the year, and only 15cm high.

It has many uses, amongst dark green dwarf conifers, between red or blue flowering plants, as an edging or even as a pot plant. Best divided in spring, it is not fussy as to soil or position, apart from a dislike of dense shade.

CARLINA ☼

Compositae

C. acaulis is a near relative of *Carduncellus*, but with multiple stemless thistle heads on low, prickly growth. The form *C. a. caulescens* has 10cm stems, and both have ivory-coloured flowers in summer. Increase by division or root cuttings.

Below: Carduncellus rhaponticoides

CERASTIUM ☼

Carophyllaceae

This genus includes the well-known but pernicious snow-in-summer. Although it makes a bright show of white flowers above grey foliage, it is so invasive that many a rock wall or garden has been ruined by it. The roots are very penetrating and almost impossible to curb or eradicate without dismantling. It should never be introduced where other choicer plants are to be grown. But there is one species worth having in C. *columnae*, which is an intensely silvery-leaved carpeter, with white flowers and a modest spread above ground.

Increased by division of well established plants in spring or autumn.

CHEIRANTHUS ☼

Cruciferae

These perennial wallflowers, some of which are perfumed, are showy. All prefer poor and dry soil to rich or moist, and will live longer in these conditions. Some are separated into the genus *Erysimum*, but are included here as being practically indistinguishable.

C. *cheiri* 'Harpur Crewe' is an old-fashioned double yellow, with sweetly-scented flowers above erect bushy growth to 35cm. C. *mutabilis* 'Constant Cheer' is basically violet-mauve, tinged amber, and is seldom out of flower, 25cm. C. 'Jacob's Jacket' is more dwarf and more spreading, with heads of multi-coloured flowers in spring and early summer. 'Moonlight' makes a low spread of greenery to 15cm, covered in lemon-yellow flowers. 'Orange Flame' is quite descriptive, as is 'Sunbright'. The last three are all low-growing and longer-lived than the first three, and autumn cuttings can be taken from all of them to renew old plants.

Cheiranthus are good wall plants as one would expect, and look attractive with cytisus and helianthemums.

Below: Cheiranthus 'Moonlight'

CHIASTOPHYLLUM

Crassulaceae

C. simplicifolia, sometimes listed as *Chiastophyllum oppositifolium* is one of the best of all rock garden plants, but it dislikes a very dry position. Otherwise it will grow in sun or shade and from rosettes of green, thinly succulent leaves sends up 15cm sprays on which dangle small, yellow flowers for many weeks. It responds to top dressing with peat or soil as an alternative to replanting more deeply every two to three years.

Easy to divide, it contrasts attractively with campanula and blue veronicas.

CHRYSANTHEMUM ☼

Compositae

A few species are sufficiently dwarf to be considered, but they bear little resemblance to the usual autumn and winter-flowering kinds. *C. hosmariense* has finely-cut, silvery leaves and will flower on and off for most of the year in a warm, sunny place or scree. Flowers are pure white, 3cm across and about 15cm high. Effective against dwarf conifers. *C. nipponicum* makes a steady spread of clumpy growth, dying back in winter. Its value is in the show of single, pink-tinged, white daisy flowers in autumn, 15–20cm. Increased by cuttings, or by division of well established plants in spring or autumn.

CHRYSOGONUM

Compositae

A single species, C. *virginianum*, which begins flowering in May and continues until autumn, with 12cm sprays of yellow flowers above leafy clumps. It is not fussy as to position in sun or shade, but needs light, non-limy soil which does not dry out. Division is easy.

Opposite: Chiastophyllum simplicifolium
Above: Chrysogonum virginianum

CODONOPSIS

Campanulaceae

These have bell-shaped flowers, like some campanulas, but are very distinctive in having exquisite markings inside the flowers, which tend to droop from lax, tenuous stems. They are unusually distinctive, and are best planted where they can hang down a bank or over a rock or wall. C. *clematidea* has light blue bells on 20–25cm stems; and C. *ovata* is somewhat similar at 15–20cm, flowering June to August.

The fleshy roots do not respond to division, but plants may be raised from seed sown under glass.

CORYDALIS ◐

Papaveraceae

Two relatively newly-introduced species are well worth growing, given the right soil and situation. *C. cashmeriana* is a little treasure for humus-rich, but gritty soil in a cool position. The flowers are of an intense sky blue, having a little head on stems only 7cm high above deeply segmented leaves of glaucous green. Plants spread slowly from tiny tuberous roots, but make an appealing display in spring. *C. flexuosa* is twice the height and is more vigorous in growth, much the same shade of blue on similar-shaped flowers, but the base foliage is of a deep purple hue. Although spring flowering, *C. flexuosa* also carries occasional flowers later in summer.

Increased by seed in autumn or division when dormant.

COTULA ☼

Compositae

These are mat-forming plants. *C. potentillina* and *squalida* are most often offered, but they are useful only for paving because of their vigorous spread of bronze-green foliage at ground level. *C. atrata* is less invasive and produces 5cm heads of browny-red and flesh pink in bicolour above the close mat of leafage. It needs well-drained soil, sun and fairly frequent replanting.

Below: Corydalis cashmereana
Below left: Corydalis flexuosa

CREPIS ☼

Compositae

Amongst a large number of weedy species are two good garden plants. The finest is C. *incana* which, with its fluffy pink flowers on 25cm stems from June to September, is a first-class plant. It has fleshy roots, which will produce root cuttings, but has no outward spread from the clump of dandelion-like foliage. C. *aurea* has upright greenery, with sprays of very deep orange flowers at 20cm from June to August.

Plants divide readily in spring.

Below: Crepis incana

CYCLAMEN ◑

Primulaceae

All the hardy cyclamen need to flourish and add interest is some shade and good drainage. Most of them have flowers at only 5–10cm high, and when in leaf these are also attractive. Corms should not be planted more than 2–3cm deep, and can be left as a permanent bed. They can only be increased by seed sown as soon as ripe.

C. *cilicium* is pink with marbled leaves; C. *purpurascens* (C. *europaeum*) has crimson, scented flowers; and C. *hederifolium* (C. *neapolitanum*) both pink and white flowers. All are late summer and autumn flowering. C. *orbiculatum* has several variations for late winter and spring flowering, and another spring flowering variety is the bright crimson, but less hardy, C. *repandum*. Cyclamen look attractive when planted with or beneath such dwarf shrubs as daphne, rhododendrons and azaleas and shrubby potentillas.

DELPHINIUM ☼

Ranunculaceae

Although the two dwarf kinds below are short-lived (two to three years), they make a bright display and can be easily reproduced from seed. D. *chinense* or *tatsienense* make erect bushy growth covered in short spikes of brightest blue from June to August, 25cm tall. D. *nudicaule* is unique for its orange-red flowers on 25cm spikes over the same period.

Both will flower in later summer from seed raised in spring, and are effective between dwarf conifers.

DIANTHUS ☼

Caryophyllaceae

These are amongst the indispensables as alpines. Most are easy to grow in light soil, but a few are best as scree plants. The latter, where the tight mounded growth makes for difficulty with cuttings, will come true from seed, and there are dwarf strains of a mixture which come quite well from seed. Otherwise, late summer cuttings or autumn division usually succeed; and all of them like a sunny position and good drainage.

There is such a wide selection of named cultivars, especially of the silvery-leaved type, growing from 5–20cm in height and flowering from June to August, that there is ample choice from catalogues or garden centres. Some make a good, close, surface mat whilst others grow more compactly.

The species *deltoides* is distinct with its trailing habit and green to bronze-purple foliage with smaller, but very bright, flowers in pink to red and glowing crimson-scarlet. Any of those with outspreading growth are adapatable for walls and slopes, and colours range from white through pink to deep red, some with double flowers.

For scree beds, slow growing, choice species include *D. alpinus* with green leaves and large, deep pink flowers, 5cm high. *D. myrtinervis* is a very compact growing *deltoides* type, with pink flowers, 4cm; *D. muralae* and *simulans* make tight mounds set with small clear pink flowers, 5cm; whilst *D. pavonius* (*D. neglectus*) has grassy tufts with quite large, rosy-red flowers. These, and others for scree, are best increased by seed.

Some of the most dwarf and choicest species, such as *D. alpinus* and *D. neglectus*, are apt to be difficult to grow, but 'Inchriach Dazzler' lives up to its name, with intense, deep pink flowers on 6–8cm stems in early summer. Given sun and good drainage it is quite reliable.

Dianthus generally fit in easily with other subjects, especially campanulas.

Below: Dianthus 'Inchriach Dazzler'

DIASCIA ☼

Scrophulariaceae

These South African subjects have become popular in recent years, with the introduction of new species and varieties. To offset a lack of complete hardiness, they are easy to grow and flower for weeks on end. *D. cordata* 'Ruby Field' is an older variety, with sprays up to 15cm bearing deep pink flowers from June to October. Combines effectively with *Gentiana septemfida*.

Some of the newcomers are rather tall to include here, but of the hybrids now available 'Salmon Supreme' is outstanding. Its sprays of open-petalled flowers are clear salmon pink, coming in long successions until late autumn. Given a sunny situation in good, well-drained soil, it will survive most winters; cuttings are easy to root and older plants easily divide. *D.* 'Lilac Belle' is about 12cm in flower.

DISPORUM ●

Liliaceae

D. oreganum (*D. smithii*) is a humus-loving, lime-hating plant which is unusual for having conspicuous, orange berries following greenish flowers. It grows erectly to 20cm, and the orange, cherry-sized berries are long lasting, nestling in the green foliage until autumn.

Old plants will divide in autumn and culture is not difficult in neutral or acid soil.

Below: Diascia cordata

DODECATHEON

Primulaceae

Natives of the USA, where they are aptly called shooting stars, these have deeply reflexed petals with prominent yellow centres. There are several species which do not vary greatly, all having long, leathery leaves and flowers hanging loosely in a clustered head, 20–25cm high, in spring. They need no special soil, but resent very dry shade. All die back to dormancy from August to March and can be increased both from seed and by division.

Colours vary a little from pink to magenta-crimson. The species *D. meadia* and *D. pulchellum* (*D. pauciflorum*) are most often offered. Effective amongst ferns, *Anemone nemorosa* and *A. ranunculoides*.

DORONICUM ◑

Compositae

Easy-to-grow plants producing large, yellow, ray-petalled flowers in spring. Some are too tall as alpines, but *D. cordatum* and *caucasicum* are only 15cm tall, as is the spring cultivar 'Goldzwerg'. There is a fully double cultivar in 'Spring Beauty' which will reach 30cm.

All flower from March well into May, and divide readily after flowering. They look pleasant with any blue or white spring flowers.

Top left: Dodecatheon meadia
Bottom left: Doronicum caucasicum

DRABA ☼

Cruciferae

All these plants are spring flowering, from March to May, and need sun and good drainage, and most of them are cushion-forming in small, green rosettes.

D. aizoides has deep green rosettes and makes a bright show of yellow flowers, 8cm. A. dedeana and salomonii are of similar habit and have white flowers. D. bruniifolia and D. repens are the easiest to grow, the latter spreading quite quickly and rooting down with short runners. Both are yellow, 5cm tall. These are all increased by division or seed.

For scree or an alpine house, D. rigida, D. imbricata and D. mollissima form very neat hummocks of slow growth, set with yellow flowers, only 3–4cm.

DRYAS ☼

Rosaceae

Mat-forming plants with leaves deep green above and silvery beneath, producing quite large white flowers of 'strawberry' formation, followed by fluffy seed heads. The best known – common in the European Alps – is D. octopetala, but this does not flower so freely as D. x suendermanii and vestita. None has flowers more than 12cm high. Dryas make good ground cover but need to be curbed. Increase by seed or cuttings in early autumn.

Above: Draba rigida

EDRAIANTHUS

Campanulaceae

The species *E. pumilio* forms tight silvery cushions set with violet-blue 5cm flowers in spring, and is best in scree soil. This is the species most often offered, but there are others a little taller and less attractive, with deep green, narrow leaves. *E. caudatus* (*E. dalmaticus*) is about the best, 15cm.

All the species are best increased by seed.

Below: Edraianthus pumilio
Opposite bottom left: Epimedium youngianum

EPILOBIUM

Onagraceae

One or two dwarf kinds of willow herb are worth growing, where not too dry. *E. glabellum* makes a loose mound of greenery and has a profusion of ivory-white flowers, 20cm, for much of the summer. *E.* 'Broadwell Hybrid' comes from a cross between this and the short lived, pink species *kaikourense*. It has purplish-bronze foliage and creamy-pink flowers, at 15cm, for many weeks.

These may be increased by seed, cuttings in early autumn or division in spring. They look attractive with campanulas and summer flowering gentians.

The species *E. macropus* should be avoided for its invasiveness.

EPIMEDIUM

Berberidaceae

The most dwarf of these are of real value in a cool position. They have very pretty foliage, forming a dome over their slowly expanding roots. Leaves are fresh until winter frost, and the display of starry flowers comes in spring, followed at once by new foliage. None is fussy as to soil, but are best where it is not too dry.

E. alpinum has rosy-purple flowers on wiry 20cm stems, whilst *rubrum* is reddish-pink. *E. grandiflorum* 'Rose Queen' grows compactly with a profusion of pink flowers only 15cm tall. The best white is *E. youngianum* 'Niveum', with a neat habit and specially good foliage.

Division is best in autumn, as the roots are quite congested and tough. Epimediums have value as edging plants to a shady path, and associate effectively with any blues, such as omphalodes and mertensia.

ERIGERON ☼

Compositae

This varied genus includes some very dwarf species, but all have the typical rayed flowers. *E. aurantiacus*, although unfortunately short lived, has bright, deep orange flowers on 20–25cm stems. Plants seldom flower for more than two seasons, but come readily from seed. *E. aureus* is also orange, only 8cm from greyish tufts and best in lime-free scree; but the tiny, violet-flowered *E. leiomerus* is tolerant of any well-drained soil. *E. simplex* makes a splendid show of pure white daisies from green, clumpy growth at 20cm. *E. mucronatus* has a profusion of pale pink and white flowers on mounded, twiggy growth for months – a good wall plant.

Apart from the last, these erigerons flower in early summer, but the hybrid 'Dimity' is at its best from June to August. This makes a sizable clump of soft green, and has arching sprays of pink, orange-flushed flowers. Though a little large for small sites, growing 20cm tall and 25cm across when in flower, it is a very showy plant.

Most erigerons are best divided in spring or after flowering, but *E. mucronatus* comes from seed, sometimes self-sown.

ERINUS ☼

Scrophulariaceae

The one species available is *E. alpinus*, which varies in colour but not in habit. The type has lilac-mauve flowers on 5–7cm spikes, and *E. a.* 'Albus' is its albino. The most popular are the pink 'Mrs Boyle' and deeper, rosy-pink 'Dr Hanelle'.

They grow in compact, non-spreading, tufted formation in any kind of soil, preferring poor soil, and will grow happily in crevices and chinks. They are not very long lived, and are easily reproduced from seed.

Below: Erinus alpinus

ERODIUM ☼

Geraniaceae

These also prefer stony soil and full sun and, in these conditions, are long lived. All have open, saucer-shaped flowers and more-or-less evergreen foliage.

E. chamaedrioides makes glossy, green tufts, studded with white pink-veined flowers for most of the summer, as does the pink-flowered E. c. 'Roseum'. Both are only 4–5cm high. E. corsicus is a little larger, with greyish leaves and deeper pink-to-red flowers, but is best in an alpine house. E. guttatum, E. macradenum and E. supracanum are much alike, all about 12cm with ferny-grey foliage and light pink flowers, prettily veined purple. Growth is a little woody, but not so much as in the beautiful E. chrysanthum, which will mound up to 20cm and carries lemon-yellow flowers.

All these are very long flowering and deep rooting plants, which can be divided with care when old or rooted from basal cuttings in a frame. They associate agreeably with sedums and zauschnerias.

ERYTHRONIUM ◗

Liliaceae

The common dog's-tooth violet is E. denscanis, which has purple-rose flowers on 15cm stems in spring, and marbled leaves. But some of the less known species are more desirable. All are spring flowering bulbs with a long dormant period from July to early March. E. californicum also has handsome, marbled leaves and large creamy flowers, 15cm tall with reflexed petals. E. x 'Pagoda' is yellow, and E. x 'White Beauty' is equally lovely.

They need a cool, but open soil and, if planted 10cm apart, will make a brave show as they increase naturally. If interplanted in spring with dwarf mimulus, the blank spaces they leave in summer will be effectively filled.

Top left: Erodium chamaedrioides 'Roseum'
Above: Erythronium x 'Pagoda'
Opposite: Euphorbia myrsinites

EUPHORBIA ☼

Euphorbiaceae

This large genus, which has a distinctive beauty, includes very few species sufficiently dwarf and compact for small sites. *E. cyparissias*, with blue-grey, low, needle-like foliage and heads of sulphur-yellow flowers, although only 15cm is apt to spread too quickly below ground. *E. myrsinites* is highly recommended for a sunny place in a very well-drained soil. It has prostrate stems from a central fleshy root, which have succulent, bluish-grey leaves all the way up to a wide head of green-tinted, golden-yellow flowers.

Euphorbia can only be perpetuated or increased by seed. Any self-sown plants which may appear should be moved into position when young. Old plants resent disturbance and will not divide. It associates well with dark-leaved dwarf conifers and hebes.

EURYOPS ☼

Compositae

E. acraeus (E. evansii) is a low, shrubby plant with silvery foliage up to 30cm tall and bright yellow, daisy flowers in summer. It needs a dry situation and is attractive over winter. Increase by seed or cuttings.

FRANKENIA ☼

Frankeniaceae

Known as the sea-heath, *F. thymifolia* makes a close carpet of deep green, only 3cm high, with a profusion of open, pink flowers from June to September. It is best in dry or sandy soil, and losses occur in cold, wet districts in winter. Increase by cuttings in summer, or division in spring.

FUCHSIA ☼

Onagraceae

Although generally classed as shrubs or indoor plants, those suitable for rock gardens can be grown outdoors. If good, pot-grown plants are obtained in spring and inserted deeply, they will survive winter frosts, especially if planted on the south side of conifers, or similar. In very cold districts, a covering of litter will give additional protection. They flower from new growth, and old stems should be cut back in spring. Increase from cuttings in summer. All flower from July onwards.

F. pumila makes neat little bushes, 15cm tall, with red and violet flowers. *F.* 'Tom Thumb' is a little taller and more robust with carmine-purple flowers at 20–25cm.

Above: Euryops acraeus
Left: Fuchsia 'Tom Thumb'
Opposite left: Genista sagittalis
Opposite right: Gentiana acaulis

GENISTA ☼

Leguminosae

All are shrubby, but some are quite prostrate and make a splendid display in early summer.

G. delphinensis is best in scree soil and has large yellow flowers on tightly congested mats, 10cm. G. pilosa spreads as twiggy, evergreen mats with masses of yellow flowers, 10cm. G. sagittalis does not flower so freely, making prostrate mats of flat stems to give evergreen and complete ground cover (like a larger G. delphinensis) and is best over a wall or bank. G. lydia is larger, more like a cytisus (broom), and is a superb wall plant with pendant sprays of light yellow flowers in early summer, 30cm. Increased from cuttings after flowering.

GENTIANA ☼ ◑

Gentianaceae

This is a name almost synonymous with alpines, and no collection is complete without some of them. They are best divided into three groups, according to flowering times. Those that flower in spring like lime in the soil, though it is not essential. They also need a sunny position, as do the summer flowering species, which will grow well in either limy or acid soil. With one exception, however, the autumn gentians will not grow in limy soil and need a cool position away from strong sun in peaty or leafy soil. All need good drainage.

G. acaulis is easy to grow, but is erratic to flower, and no sure way of enticing it to flower profusely and regularly has been

found. It makes clumpy growth of ever-green rosettes at ground level. The rich blue, trumpet flowers appear in **spring**, 10cm. Clumps will divide, but need to be planted very firmly. They combine happily with drabas, dianthus and erinus.

G. *verna* is much smaller, with more open flowers of intense blue. It needs scree soil, and appreciates the addition of cow manure. It is best increased by seed sown under glass after being frozen. The **summer** gentians are easy in any reasonable soil. The species G. *septemfida* is most often offered, flowering from June to August with loosely held blue trumpets to about 20cm. There are other species akin to this – mostly good garden plants, but not easy to divide and best raised from seed.

Autumn gentians, the lime haters, grow with white, thong-like roots and have narrow, grassy foliage stems terminating in blue trumpets from August to October, at about 12cm. Shades of blue vary from electric blue in the one lime-tolerant species G. *farreri*, to the deeper blue variations and hybrids of the best known G. *sino-ornata*. The roots will fall apart for division, and it is beneficial to replant in the spring every two or three years. Do not plant where the soil can dry out or bake; and for a group, they can be planted only 10cm apart. These late gentians are ideal for peat bed cultivation.

Below left: Gentiana septemfida
Below: Gentiana sino-ornata

GERANIUM ☼ ◑

Geraniaceae

The most dwarf of these true, hardy geraniums are invaluable for their adaptability, long life and long flowering.

G. dalmaticum, in both shell pink and white, flowers in May and June from clumpy growth, 10cm. *G. cinerium*, with ash-grey foliage and pink flowers, is less often seen than the hybrids 'Apple Blossom', light pink, and 'Ballerina' with large, open, lilac-pink flowers, prettily veined crimson. Both are 10cm and deservedly popular, flowering from June to September. *G. farreri* (*G. napuligerum*) needs a scree soil to give of its best; stems are red and flowers soft pink with black centres, 10cm, June to August.

G. sanguineum is best in the form 'Lancastriense', which is more compact with mounded growth up to 15cm, covered in clear pink, open flowers. This is extra good when topping a retaining wall, as is the vivid magenta-purple *G. cinerium subcaulescens* at a similar height. The two go well together, especially if interplanted with blue campanula. A less vigorous *G. c. subcaulescens* is the warm pink *G. c. s.* 'Splendens'. *G. sessiliflorum nigricans* makes a low cushion of small brown leaves, set with near-white flowers.

Most of these hardy geraniums have woody roots, but old plants can be divided.

GEUM ☼

Rosaceae

Only two are sufficiently dwarf to include. Both are easy to grow, flowering in early summer, and can be divided in early autumn. *G. x. borisii* has deep, bright orange flowers to 20cm, above soft green, leafy clumps. *G. rossii*, quite different, has carrot-like leaves and yellow flowers, 20cm. Both combine pleasantly with *Veronica teucrium* or *rupestris*.

Below: Geranium cinerium 'Ballerina'
Overleaf top: Geranium c. subcaulescens
  'Splendens'
Overleaf bottom: Geranium dalmaticum

GLOBULARIA ☼

Globulariaceae

These are true alpines and of value in small sites, with low tufts of dark, evergreen leaves. Flowers come as little blue, fluffy balls in early summer. *G. incanescens* is a choice species, best in scree conditions, with flowers of bright powder blue, only 7cm high. *G. cordifolia* and *G. meridionalis* (*G. bellidifolia*) are a little larger, of easy growth at 10cm; whilst *G. trichosantha* and *G. elongata* are more robust in growth, at 15–20cm.

Old plants are best divided in early autumn or spring.

GYPSOPHILA ☼

Caryophyllaceae

These are trailing plants, some too large for small sites, but nonetheless excellent for walls or where they can hang down. They are long flowering, and long lived.

G. cerastioides is distinct for not having a trailing habit, but makes low mounds set with whitish-pink flowers. One of the finest trailing plants is *G. dubia*, which makes a splendid display with bluish-grey foliage and sheets of clear pink flowers. *G. repens* (*G. fratensis*) is very similar, as is G. 'Dorothy Teacher', though this is a little larger at 10cm. *G. repens*, and its forms 'Alba' and 'Monstrosa', is rather rampant. So is G. 'Rosy Veil', but its spread only lasts a season, as it dies back in autumn to a strong, deep rootstock. It is a good plant for a bank or wall top.

All can be increased by cuttings or division.

Top right: Globularia incanescens
Bottom right: Gypsophila dubia

HABERLEA ●

Gesneraceae

These are plants for cool shade, but not for growing under trees. A north-facing aspect is best, preferably with the plants' leafy rosettes resting on or between stones. They also prefer leaf-mould or peaty soil. *H. ferdinandi-coburgii* has soft lilac-blue flowers on short, branching stems, 10cm high, in May and June. *H. rhodopensis* has somewhat similar flowers of lavender-lilac; and there is a white form of this named *H. r.* 'Virginalis'.

Haberleas can be divided in late summer, and look fine with ferns, dicentra and dodecatheon.

HACQUETIA ◑

Umbelliferae

The one species available at present, *H. epipactis*, is best in some shade and is included, not only because it grows well in dampish or heavy soil and is long lived, but also because it flowers in earliest spring. The flowers are in sulphur-yellow heads, 15cm tall, and when these are over a low canopy of green leaves comes from its tough, clumpy roots. An attractive variegated form is expected to be available shortly.

Division is best in autumn and it is quite adaptable, and for peat beds as well.

HAPLOPAPPUS ☼

Compositae

H. lyallii makes 15cm mounds, on which deep yellow flowers come on short stems in later summer, when most alpines are less colourful. The green leaves are deeply toothed. It needs very well-drained soil in full sun, and is effective on top of a wall. Propagate from cuttings or division in spring.

Below: Hacquetia epipactis

HELIANTHEMUM ☼

Cistaceae

The so-called rock roses, though somewhat shrubby, are included here as they are very popular and are considered to be indispensible alpines. Most of those offered are cultivars in a wide variety of names and colours, from whites to pinks, yellows, reds, orange-brown and many intermediate and bicolour shades. Some are also double flowered, and many have silvery foliage. Some are of prostrate growth while others are more rounded up to 25cm in height, but all respond to clipping back after their early summer flowering has ended. This encourages tidiness as some are of quite vigorous growth, and may result in a second flowering in late summer. None is difficult to grow and all will flourish in quite dry or poor soil, their only dislike being of wet conditions. All will come easily from cuttings under a frame, which are best taken after flowering or in early autumn.

Only two distinctive species need be mentioned. *H. lunulatum* makes erect little greyish bushes about 20cm, covered in small, pure yellow flowers over a long period. *H. serpyllifolium* is also yellow, but its green growth is completely prostrate and it flowers in May and June. The form 'Chocolate Blotch' has orange-brown flowers, 'Wisley Pink' clear pink flowers and 'Annabel' double, light pink flowers.

Helianthemums are so varied in form and colour that they benefit from association with blue-flowered plants to give the complete spectrum.

Above: Helianthemum 'Annabel'

HELICHRYSUM

Compositae

Some of these are also shrubby, but have outstanding silvery foliage which lasts the year round. All are best in gritty, well-drained soil for maximum possible survival, but a few are somewhat too tender for cold districts.

H. bellidioides is mat-forming with white, crispy flowers on 10cm stems. It is of vigorous growth and fully hardy, as is the charming H. milfordiae (H. marginatum). This makes a mat of silvery rosettes with stemless, crimson-flecked, white flowers in late spring. Both are easy to divide for replanting. H. virgineum has larger rounded leaves, felted and silvery, with buff-pink flower buds opening to creamy white on 20cm stems, in May and June. H. frigidum and a few others are best as alpine house plants, attractive the year round; but the tiny grey shrublet H. selago is more adaptable given gritty soil and full sun. It grows somewhat like a bushy tree cactus with tiny yellow flowers to 15cm.

HEPATICA

Ranunculaceae

In nature these are semi-woodland plants, but are adaptable to more open situations with some shade. They do not dislike lime, and are as happy in stiff loam as in a peaty mixture. Hepaticas expand very slowly, and are also slow from seed. Division is seldom needed, although they can be divided when old but may take a year or two to settle down again.

H. nobilis (H. triloba) has small but bright, open flowers to 15cm in March, followed by a canopy of ivy-like leaves. The type is blue, with white and pink less commonly seen, and there are some very rare and beautiful double forms of each. H. transsilvanica (H. angulosa) is a little later, with lighter blue flowers and trilobed leaves of a lighter green; 'Loddon Blue' is a good cultivar.

Below left: Helichrysum milfordiae
Below: Hepatica nobilis
Opposite top: Hieracium villosum
Opposite bottom: Hepatica nobilis

HIERACIUM ☼

Compositae

Some species are weeds, but two are good garden plants for any sunny position. *H. villosum* has woolly, silvery leaves and a bright display of yellow, dandelion-type flowers on 20cm stems in summer. It is easy to divide, or from seed. *H. waldsteinii* forms rosetted clumps of soft, silvered leaves and has sprays of yellow flowers, 35cm. Unlike *villosum*, this retains its foliage over winter.

HIPPOCREPIS ☼

Leguminosae

The cultivar 'E R Janes' of *H. comosa* is an excellent carpeter for a sunny place and well-drained, limy soil. The green mats are covered in late spring with lemon yellow, pea-shaped flowers, at only 5cm. Increased by division of well established plants in spring or autumn.

HORMINUM ☼

Labiatae

H. pyrenaicum is an evergreen, rosette-forming plant with crinkled leaves making a mat of growth, though not invasive. It will grow in any garden soil, and is easily divided. The small, deep blue flowers come on 15–20cm stems in June and July. There is a deep pink variation 'Roseum'. This is not a startling plant, but it is trouble free.

Overleaf: Hippocrepis comosa 'E R Janes'

HOSTA ◐ ●

Funkiaceae

The plantain lilies have become deservedly popular garden plants, but only a few are sufficiently dwarf to include as alpines. They have both flowers and ornamental leaves, and prefer shade. *H. minor* 'Alba' has pointed green leaves and pure white flowers in late summer, 20cm high. *H. undulata* 'Medio Variegata' has wavy-edged, green leaves with prominent yellowish streaks and 35cm flower spikes of mauve trumpets. *H. tardiflora* is amongst the smallest growing species and latest to flower. The lavender-mauve flowers come in September on 20cm stems.

Hostas respond to good, moist soil with peat which can be used as a mulch. Plants can be left alone for years, or they may be divided in early spring.

Below: Hutchinsia alpina

HUTCHINSIA ◑

Cruciferae

Demure, evergreen, cushion-forming plants preferring a cool position. The leaves are dark shiny green, deeply divided, and the white flowers come as dainty sprays on 8cm stems. *H. alpina* is most often seen, but *H. auerswaldii* is even more compact at 5cm. Both flower in May and June, and can be divided in early autumn.

HYDROCOTYLE ☼

Umbelliferae

H. moschata is a rapid spreading carpeter, included only for its use as a paving plant. The flowers are of no consequence, but the leaves are tiny, bright green rosettes. Increased by division of well established plants in spring or autumn.

HYLOMECON

Papaveraceae

H. vernalis (H. japonicum) is a charming, unusual spring flowering plant for any cool soil or position. The flowers come in April and May amid pleasantly green foliage, and are as open, golden poppies, 3–6cm across. The fleshy roots are apt to become congested with age, but are easily divided and replanted after flowering or in autumn.

HYPERICUM

Hypericaceae

A genus which includes well-known shrubs and good alpine plants, some of which lack hardiness. The hardiest are those which are also excellent for wall tops or in crevices, and include *H. olympicum* – often listed as *polyphyllum* (or *fragile*). The flowers are bright yellow with prominent stamens, and in *H. o.* 'Grandiflorum' they are golden yellow and 2cm across. All this type have glaucous foliage and woody growth, and flower from June to August, mounding up to 25cm. And of the type, the lemon-yellow *H.* 'Citrinum' should not be omitted. *H. coris* is of much neater habit, forming little erect bushes of dark green to about 15cm, and producing starry, golden flowers for many weeks from June onwards.

Others, less hardy and best in scree in warm districts or in an alpine house where cold, are the creeping *H. reptans* and *H. trichocaulon*, both deep yellow, 5cm. *H. cerastoides (H. rhodopaeum)* is quite hardy with clumpy, upright, glaucous-leaved stems and light yellow flowers.

Hypericums are best from summer cuttings under glass, or from seed, with the exception of *H. coris*, which will divide.

HYPSELA

Campanulaceae

H. reniformis (H. longiflora) is an easy-to-grow, creeping plant, making close, green growth at ground level and bearing little, pinkish-white flowers for several weeks in summer. A good paving plant or in shady crevices. Increased by division of well established plants in spring autumn.

Left: Hypericum coris

IBERIS ☼

Cruciferae

The hardiest of these are all white flowered, but are outstandingly showy. The general habit is of low, dense, shrubby, evergreen growth which is covered with rounded heads of pure white in spring. *I. sempervirens* and *I. commutatum* are evergreen and excellent for a wall top, long-living and capable of hanging over with little or no attention. *I.* 'Snowflake' is more upright and mound-forming to 25cm, with fine white heads from May to July. Both this and *I.* 'Little Gem' are more compact, but the latter is bushier at 15cm. Division is possible, but summer cuttings produce better plants.

I. saxatilis is best in scree or as a trough plant. It is slow growing and quite prostrate, and covers itself in white flowers only 3cm high. Increase only by cuttings.

Below: Iberis commutatum

IRIS ☼

Iridaceae

Several dwarf species are valuable for various situations and soils. *I. chamaeris* is also listed as *I. pumila* and, as a group, they are like miniature bearded or June-flowering iris. They flower in April and May at heights ranging from 15 to 30cm, and are available in several named varieties. Their colours range from white to pink, and cream and yellow as well as blue and violet. Whilst their flowering period is rather brief, they can provide colour where their inclusion is not in conflict with purist views on alpine plants.

I. clarkei is a true species with neat erect foliage and bright blue, flecked and spotted flowers in June at 25cm. *I. cristata* needs a cool, moist soil to produce its dainty blue flowers at 15cm, but the form *I. c. lacustris* is only half the size. *I. graminea* tends to hide its scented, 15cm high reddish-purple flowers amid grassy foliage. *I. innominata* comes in

variable colour, apricot yellow in the type, but in amongst these appear lilac, purple and lavender. This species dislikes lime, as does the somewhat similar *I. tencea* with lavender-blue flowers; both reach 20cm in height, and flower in May and June. Seed raised plants are better than from divisions.

Otherwise, all the above can be divided and replanted after flowering; and they associate effectively with primulas, campanulas and mimulus.

One needs to be cautious in using bulbs as alpines. Some, with a rapid spread or increase, can become a nuisance, whilst others leave a bare patch after flowering. *I. danfordei* and *reticulata* make a brave show in early spring, but are best over-planted with creeping thymes.

JASIONE ☼

Campanulaceae

Easy and attractive plants in the somewhat similars species of *J. jankae* and *J. perennis*. They form evergreen, rosetted tufts which bear rounded, fluffy blue heads on 15–20cm stems, from June to August. Any ordinary soil suits these and they can be divided or reared from seed.

Above: Lamium maculatum 'Aureum'
Opposite: Leontopodium alpinum

LAMIUM ◑ ●

Labiatae

Most of these are much too invasive for rock gardens, though useful for ground cover in shade. There are, however, two non-rampant kinds which prefer both shade and good soil. *L. garganicum* forms leafy clumps set with clear pink flowers, 20cm, for many weeks of summer. *L. maculatum* 'Aureum' is a plant used for its foliage of rich golden hue rather than for its pink flowers, 15cm. Although neither of these run about, as does *L. maculatum* in its other forms, they expand steadily and may need curbing after two to three years. Increased by division of well established plants in spring or autumn.

LEONTOPODIUM ☼

Compositae

The genus includes the true edelweiss *L. alpinum* with its grey leaves and curiously attractive white flowers. Although easy to grow, it is seldom long lived in the type and is reproduced from seed. There are various forms which are more reliably perennial but not quite so conspicuous in flower, including *L. crassum* and *souleii* and the pleasantly lemon-scented *L. aloysiodorum*. Height 20cm.

LIMONIUM ☼

Plumbaginaceae

The miniature species of sea lavender are suitable subjects, but make no bright display with their tiny, deep blue flowers. Plants are of tufted, deep green, leathery leaves and short sprays in later summer. *L. cosyrense*, which can only be increased by seed, is 12–15cm tall: and *L. bellidifolia* has violet flowers on 20cm stems.

LINARIA ☼

Scrophulariaceae

These are not very long lived plants, but will reproduce easily from seed. They have a long flowering season, however, and are easy to grow. *L. alpina* has blue-grey, fragile stems and leaves, with small, bright flowers, mostly violet and yellow bicolour and sometimes pink and yellow, 5cm high. *L. origanifolia* grows to 20cm, with deep violet and white flowers.

LINUM ☼

Linaceae

These sun-loving plants make little spread from the roots, but vary considerably with bright yellow, blue and white open flowers from May to August. They are best in dry soil, dislike winter wet and are increased by seed.

    L. perenne (*L. alpina*) has quite large, salver-shaped blue flowers above narrow 20cm foliage. *L. arboreum* forms a low, bluish leaved, shrubby mound with flowers of pure yellow, 20cm. *L. flavum* is similar, but green leaved and less shrubby, 20–25cm. *L. suffruticosum salsoloides* is white and best in its dwarf form 'Nanum', growing almost prostrate and of similar habit to the charming light blue *L. extraaxillare.*

LIRIOPE ☼ ◑

Liliaceae

These long lived plants with grassy, ever-green leaves are widely adaptable for sun or partial shade in any but wet, heavy soils.

    L. graminifolia is mat forming, useful only for ground cover as the flowers are insignificant. The bladed leaves are dark green, and plants spread steadily. *L. hyacinthiflora* (*Reineckia carnea*) has more upright grassy foliage, half hiding the tiny spikes of fragrant flowers in April and May, 25cm high. The most colourful flowers are seen in *L. muscari* which, though a trifle tall, grows compactly into a large, mounded clump with arching, deep green blades. The lilac-purple flowers come freely in close-set spikes, 30–35cm, in late summer and autumn when colour is scarce. These

Top left: Linum arboreum
Left: Liriope muscari

plants, though dividable, can be left alone for years. A dwarfed cultivar is *L.* 'Majestic', but this needs a hot, dry place to induce its lilac-purple flowers to make a show.

LITHOSPERMUM ☼

Boraginaceae

The cultivars 'Heavenly Blue' or 'Grace Ward' of *L. diffusum* make a brilliant display of blue where the soil is lime free. The deep green leaves on prostrate stems are slightly hairy, and the open blue flowers bloom from May to July or August. Plants will not divide, but will come from cuttings in summer under glass – which is sometimes necessary when old plants become exhausted. They are attractive where they can spread over a wall, and are happy in a sunny position or in a peat bed. They associate well with dianthus and hypericums.

L. oleifolium is more upright with greyish leaves and large, sky blue flowers, but it needs a sheltered position or to be grown in an alpine house, 15cm, May and June. *Lithodora zahnii*, a miniature evergreen of mounded habit, carries small, blue flowers in May and June.

Below left: Lithospermum diffusum
   'Heavenly Blue'
Below: Lithodora zahnii

LYCHNIS ○

Caryophyllaceae

Although some species are truly alpine and brightly coloured, a few are so short lived that they are little more than annuals. They are all easy to grow in any well-drained soil.

L. flos-jovis 'Hort's Variety' makes soft silvery tufts and 20cm spikes of brightest pink flowers in early summer. L. x arkwrightii is outstanding for its brilliant vermilion flowers above deep purple foliage, about 25cm tall. It is a cultivar from L. x haageana of similar colour but with green leaves. L. viscaria has deep green tufts and sticky stems carrying pink flowers (or white in L. v. 'Alba'), but the showiest is L. v. 'Splendens Plena'. This has large, double pink flowers like a small carnation, on 25cm stems in June and July, and will divide in early autumn or spring. But the others are best from seed; as are the two short lived species having bright pink flowers, L. alpina and L. lagascae (Petrocoptis glaucifolia). Both are only 10cm and flower from May to July.

All like sandy or light soil and associate pleasantly with campanulas.

LYSIMACHIA ◑ ●

Primulaceae

L. nummularia 'Aurea' is the only worthwhile species, being the golden leaved form of creeping jenny. It needs a cool shady place where its trailing stems, with occasional yellow flowers, can wander and root down. Any excessive spread is easily checked. Increased by division of well established plants in spring or autumn.

Below: Lychnis viscaria 'Splendens Plena'
Opposite: Mentha requienii

MAZUS ◑

Scrophulariaceae

The two species are both good carpeting plants for any but the driest situations. *M. pumilio* has stemless, lavender-blue and white bicolour flowers above close green foliage, only 2–3cm; while *M. reptans* (*M. rugosus*) has mauve and white flowers with bronzy-green leaves. Both are so filmy that they can be used for paving and as cover plants for bulbs. Increased by division of well established plants in spring or autumn.

MENTHA ◑

Labiatae

M. requienii is of even smaller filmy growth with tiny rounded leaves and almost microscopic lavender-blue flowers. Its other distinction is the strong mint aroma which a touch or tread will induce. It is not hardy everywhere, but in most districts enough usually survives to spread quickly again in summer in any cool position. Other menthas are too large or rampant to be included. Increased by division of well established plants in spring or autumn.

MERTENSIA ☽

Boraginaceae

Only three species are sufficiently dwarf
and all prefer a shady position, though they
are not difficult to grow. They are mat
forming, with rounded or tongue-shaped
leaves which fade in autumn. In spring
come sprays of intense blue flowers, mid-
blue in *M. primuloides* and violet-blue in *M.
coventryana*. The latter has a fairly rapid
spread, and all respond to mulching. *M.
asiatica* is of trailing habit with bluish leaves
set with small purple-blue flowers. Increased by seed, or division of well established
plants in spring or autumn.

MICROMERIA ☀

Labiatae

These are very dwarf and somewhat
shrubby plants. They all have aromatic
foliage and are best grown in light soil and
full sun. *M. corsica* makes tight, silvery
hummocks 5cm high, set with tiny, bright
pink flowers which last for many weeks. *M.
illyrica* has dark green foliage and blue
flowers in later summer, 15cm. Plants can
be divided in spring.

MIMULUS ☀

Scrophulariaceae

Notable for having lipped, trumpet-shaped
flowers in brilliant colours. All the mimulus
below like moist but not boggy soil, and
mainly sunny situations. Most of them
form shallow rooting mats, which are best
divided and replanted in enriched soil in late

summer or spring. A few can be raised from
seed sown under glass, and they will also
come from summer cuttings of basal
growth.

 M. cupreus is the parent of most of the
colourful, named cultivars with a mat-
forming growth. *M. burnetii* has brown-
orange flowers on 20cm stems, and *M.
langsdorffii* is of similiar height with pure,
bright yellow flowers. *M.* 'Puck' is dwarf
and free flowering with buff-yellow
flowers. Bicolour flowers in maroon and
yellow come in *M.* 'Shep'. At 15cm, 'Wisley
Red' is more dwarf and very showy; and
'Whitecroft Scarlet', at only 10cm, is nearer
vermilion in colour. These last two are
much less vigorous but, as with the others,
it is a good plan to cut back after the first
June to July flowering and top dress with
fertilised sandy peat, to promote new basal
growth which may result in a second
flowering. The diminutive yellow species
M. primuloides is pretty but not fully hardy.

 Mimulus associate successfully with the
taller primulas and dwarf astilbes, but are
not suitable for raised beds.

Above: Mertensia asiatica
Opposite top: Mimulus burnetii 'A T Johnson'
Opposite: Mimulus 'Puck'

MITELLA ◐ ●

Saxifragaceae

These are grown more for their evergreen foliage cover than for their tiny, brownish-green sprays of flowers. The plants make leafy mounds 10cm high, and are amongst the few kinds equally at home in quite dry soil in shade as in more open positions. *M. breweri* has glossy, mounded foliage and 15cm flower sprays, and *M. caulescens* has a quicker spread closer to the surface, in light green. The latter will give cover to bulbs, and both are easy to divide.

MOLTKIA ☼

Boraginaceae

M. intermedia (formerly known as *Lithospermum intermedium*) is a splendid subject for a sunny place and gritty soil, and does not object to lime. It mounds up to 20cm and has short sprays of small, bright blue flowers from May to July. Increased by basal cuttings or careful division.

MORISIA ☼

Cruciferae

M. monanthos (*M. hypogaea*) is rewarding for its bright yellow flowers in spring, almost at ground level from a compact tuft of green, jagged leaves. It needs scree or well-drained soil, and is excellent in troughs with *Gentiana verna* for company. Propogation is by root cuttings in early spring.

Right: Morisia monanthos

MYOSOTIS ☼

Boraginaceae

M. rupicola is a little forget-me-not, which is perennial though seldom living beyond three years. The flowers are intensely blue, on 10cm sprays from a leafy tuft, from April to June. This, too, needs gritty soil and is useful for troughs. Comes true from seed.

OENOTHERA ☼

Onagraceae

A genus which embraces both perennial and biennial species and includes the evening primrose.

The best dwarf perennials have a long display of yellow flowers, except for *O. taraxacifolia* which has large, shaggy, white, pink-tinged flowers on prostrate stems with jagged leaves. This is best in poor, dry

soil and is renewed from seed, as is *O. acaulis* which has stemless yellow flowers. Both flower from June to August. Also for a dry, open soil but with too much summer spread for confined spaces is the splendid *O. missouriensis*. Although its fangy roots do not spread, a single plant can cover a wide area with prostrate, leafy growth. The flowers from June to September are large, reddish in the bud but pure lemon yellow when open. An excellent plant for a dry, sunny slope.

O. caespitosa has neat, clumpy growth with large white flowers on short stems, whilst *O. riparia* has a leafy, mounded spread of about 30cm across and 20cm tall, with pure yellow flowers, June to September. *O. glaber* has rich golden-yellow flowers 4–5cm across on 30cm stems with bronzy-foliage, and is attractive and reliable if not too tall. These tufty species are best divided in spring.

OMPHALODES ◑

Boraginaceae

These are carpeting plants showing kinship with myosotis, and the ones below are fully perennial and good carpeters in any ordinary soil. *O. cappadocica* is evergreen, with ribbed grey-green leaves and sprays of bright blue flowers in spring. *O. c.* 'Anthea Bloom' is very free flowering in sky blue. Both are 15cm tall, flourish with minimal attention for several years with slow spread and are best divided in early autumn. *O. verna*, seen in both blue and white, is more rampant and does not retain its leaves beyond summer. It flowers briefly in April, 10cm. All respond to an occasional light mulch.

Top right: Oenothera missouriensis
Right: Omphalodes cappadocica

ONOSMA ☼

Boraginaceae

The best known of this small genus is *O. tauricum*. It has hairy, narrow leaves of grey-green forming a mound from a tap root and needs well-drained soil. The flowers are light yellow and tubular, dangling from 25cm stems, May to July. Seed is the only means of continuity when plants are exhausted. A pink-tinged species of similar growth is *O. albo-roseum*.

OPHIOPOGON ◗

Liliaceae

These are closely related to liriope and have evergreen, grassy foliage and short spikes of tiny purple flowers in summer. The most outstanding is *O. planiscapus nigrescens* with almost black, 10cm foliage. It makes a slow spread from underground shoots, and can be left alone for years except for an occasional mulching for peat. The green *O. planiscapus* is useful only for ground cover, and tiny spikes of white flowers, 10cm, nestle in the narrow, green leaves of *O. japonicus*. The variegated form is less hardy.

Increased by division of well established plants in spring or autumn.

ORIGANUM ☼

Labiatae

These are distinctive for having nepeta-like flowers in late summer. The most attractive need a very well-drained soil and resent winter wet. *O. hybridum* has woolly, grey-green leaves from a compact root, and wiry sprays carrying rosy-purple flowers, July to September, 15–20cm tall. *O. scabrum pulchrum* is quite sturdy, forming clumpy plants on which appear a profusion of pale pink, green-tinged bracts in late summer, 15cm. The large, hop-like flowers of *O. rotundifolia* are creamy green on 12cm stems. All are long lived where suited, and can be divided in spring.

OURISIA ◑

Scrophulariaceae

Mat-forming plants for moist or peaty soil which does not dry out. *O. coccinea* has bright green leaves from surface-rooting plants, and scarlet flowers dangling from 20cm stems at intervals during summer. It is not very free flowering, and appreciates a top dressing of peat. Not hardy in very cold areas. *O. macrophylla* is also a little tender with dense, deep green, rounded leaves and a striking display of pure white flowers in early summer. Both are easy to divide.

OXALIS ☼ ◑

Oxalidaceae

A genus which includes two or three species of troublesome weeds, as well as some good garden plants. *O. adenophylla* has tufts of crumply grey leaves and larger, funnel-shaped flowers of lilac-pink in late spring, 5cm. This and the white *O. enneaphylla* are best in scree or gritty soil. *O. inops* is pretty, but should be avoided as it is invasive; and *O. magellanica* makes a neat carpet of bronzy, lobed leaves and small, round white flowers for much of the summer, 3cm. It is best in a less sunny, moist position.

O. articulata (floribunda) is happy in dry soil and is very adaptable. It makes a mound of shamrock-like, year round greenery, and 15cm stems carry a loose head of bright pink flowers from May to August. The roots are like congested corms, but are easily divided.

Opposite left: Ophiopogon planiscapus nigrescens
Opposite: Origanum scabrum pulchrum

PAPAVER ☼

Papaveraceae

Two diminutive species of poppy are worthy of note, in spite of being short lived. *P. alpinum* grows like a miniature Iceland poppy (*P. nudicaule*) with single flowers rising to 12cm from a blue-green tuft, May to August, in white, yellow and orange shades. *P. miyabeanum* makes a mound of lobed, greyish leaves and has a long succession of soft, light yellow flowers, 10cm. Seed is the only means of reproduction of both the above, and they often self-sow.

PARAHEBE ☼

Scrophulariaceae

This name has now been given to some sub-shrubby hebes, all of which formerly came under *Veronica*. *P. catarractae* makes low mounds of dark green, shiny leaves and pale lilac flowers in early summer, 25cm. The form 'Diffusus' is dwarfed at 15cm, and more desirable. *P. lyallii* is more upright at 15–20cm with near-white flowers, and 'Miss Willmott' is of similar height with pinkish-lilac flowers. The taller ones respond to trimming with shears after flowering, but *P. bidwillii*, with bronzy leaves and a few white flowers, is too small to need this, being only 5cm.

Parahebes can be divided and combine agreeably with most penstemons.

PENSTEMON ☼

Scrophulariaceae

This varied genus includes both dwarf

herbaceous and some shrubby species. The latter, especially, need a sunny place and sharp drainage.

P. alpinus forms clumps of broad leaves and has 20cm spikes of light blue flowers in May and June. P. barrattae is of similar height with blue-purple, tubular flowers; and P. virens has small, but intensely deep blue flowers on 15cm spikes above green-leaved mats. These three are non-shrubby and can be divided or reared from seed.

The shrubby kinds may also come from seed, but are better from cuttings after flowering. The erect growing P. heterophyllus 'Blue Gem' has very showy, sky-blue spikes to 20cm. This comes only from seed. P. edithae has large, purple-rose flowers on low 25cm bushes. P. pinifolius grows erectly with narrow leaves and sprays of scarlet flowers, 20cm. 'Mersea Yellow' a pleasing variation, is also long flowering. P. roezlii is low growing at 15cm with deep red flowers, and is effective in or on a wall. P. scouleri has light lavender flowers, 20cm; and the cultivar 'Six Hills' has large, soft lilac flowers, 10–15cm.

Shrubby penstemons respond to top dressing with sandy soil in which new roots can form, but if they appear to be losing vigour it is advisable to take cuttings or sometimes to replant more deeply. Several other species are in cultivation.

PHLOX ☼ ◑

Polemoniaceae

The easiest and most popular kinds come under the species P. douglasii or P. subulata. Both are carpeters and capable of rooting as they spread. They are invaluable for making a bright display in spring and early summer, and are especially effective on a slope as they need no special soil or attention, given good drainage and a mainly sunny position. Those under P. douglasii have a colour range from white to lilac, pale blue and pink, with close growing mats of small leaves and flowers and are generally of neat habit, to a height of 5cm. In P. subulata there are some brighter colours, including crimson red, which are available amongst the twenty or so cultivars in existence. Most of them have a quicker spread than P. douglasii and flower at about 8cm high.

Few alpine phlox need shade and peaty or acid soil, although P. adsurgens prefers these conditions. It has small, leathery leaves and heads of soft pink flowers. This is not an easy plant, in contrast to P. amoena which is undemanding in a sunny position. Its growth is more tufted, though still mat-forming with magenta-pink flower heads, and there is also a pretty, variegated-leaved form. P. stolonifera spreads quickly, with blue, pink or white flowers and self-rooting rosettes or runners with rounded leaves. It flowers in spring at 10cm and is best in cool soil and some shade, as is P. divaricata (P. canadensis). P. d. laphami has loose heads of clear lavender-blue flowers in May and June, 15cm, and prefers a soil enriched with peat or leaf-mould.

All the above may be increased from cuttings.

Left: Penstemon pinifolius 'Mersea Yellow'
Opposite top: Phlox douglasii 'Crackerjack'
Opposite: Phlox subulata

PHYLLITIS ◑ ●

Polypodiaceae

P. scolopendrium is the well-known hart's tongue fern. It is not out of place in a rocky wall with some shade, and the variations 'Cristata' and 'Undulata' (crested and wavy edged) are most attractive. They are not fussy as to soil and are long lived. Increased by division of well established plants in spring or autumn.

PHYTEUMA ☼

Campanulaceae

These have distinctive blue flower heads with sharply pointed petals. The best known *P. comosum* is a good little plant, only 8cm, and happy in a crevice between rocks. It has lilac-blue flowers, as has the taller *P.*

orbiculare. Both are easy to grow. *P. scheuchzeri* has deep purple flowers on 20cm stems. All flower in spring and early summer, and are best perpetuated by seed.

POLEMONIUM ☼ ◑

Polemoniaceae

Only a few of the Jacob's ladders can be included. All have divided leaves (from which the folk name is derived), and sprays of small, open, cup-shaped flowers in early summer. *P. pauciflorum* has ferny leaves and pendant, light yellow flowers, 15cm tall. *P. reptans* is both vigorous and adaptable; the best in the cultivar, 'Blue Pearl', making a bright but rather brief display of blue flowers in May and June, 20cm. Increased by division of well established plants in spring or autumn.

Below: Phyteuma comosum

POLYGALA ☼ ◐

Polygalaceae

The non-shrubby *P. calcarea* forms a tidy mat of dark green, covered with brilliant blue flowers in early summer, 5cm high, and is a good scree plant for limy soils, sometimes reproducing itself from seed. In contrast, two other somewhat shrubby species are strictly for acid, peaty soil. *P. chamaebuxus* is a low, evergreen bush, 12cm high. In the type the pea-shaped flowers are cream and yellow, but in *P. c* 'Purpurea' they are maroon and yellow, whilst in *P. c.* 'Grandi-flora' they are deep pink and gold. They flower from April to June and, though not adaptable, make a good display where suited. *P. vayredae* is not spectacular with narrow foliage to 15cm, and small purplish flowers.

Polygalas look fine in association with erythroniums, and are increased by division of well established plants in spring or autumn.

POLYGONUM ☼ ◐

Polygonaceae

This large genus is immensely varied in form and requirements. Some are weedy, but those below are good garden plants.

P. affine is variable and as a type is best for giving both flowers and ground cover, away from slow growing plants. The pink, pokery spikes are up to 20cm. *P.a.* 'Donald Lowndes' is a good, free flowering form and 'Darjeel-ing Red' has thinner, deep rose spikes. They flower at intervals during the summer and autumn. They are of rapid surface-rooting growth, sometimes dying out in patches and needing replanting.

Right: Polygonum vaccinifolium

'Dimity' has a compact leafy spread with 20cm pink spikes. *P. tenuicaule* is spring flowering with little 10cm spikes of white from a clumpy plant, best in moist soil. *P. vaccinifolium* is a splendid late flowering species and, although a little invasive, it is easily curbed. The congested, twiggy mat covers itself with slender spikes of bright rose pink in sun or shade, 10cm high. It is, however, more at home in non-limy soil.

Where scope permits, the newly dis-covered is worth having. *P. amplexicaule* 'Arun Gem' has dangling pokers of bright pink and a neat habit. Although 30–40cm tall, it is charmingly graceful and flowers from July till cut back to a compact root by frost. It grows in any good soil in sun or partial shade, and can be divided.

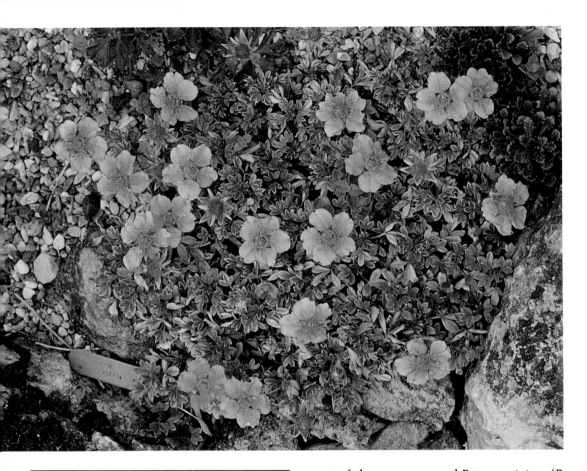

POTENTILLA ☼

Rosaceae

These showy, easily grown plants will succeed in any reasonable soil and, although preferring sun, do not object to some partial shade. The popular, shrubby kind are too large for most rock gardens, but the same open-petalled flowers in similar colours are represented on the more dwarf types of tufted, clumpy or mat-forming habit, all of which are easy to divide when they become old and less free to flower.

P. aurea forms green, prostrate mats with ample, golden flowers in summer, and there is a double flowered form of this, both at 5cm. P. alba is white, more tufted and 15cm tall. P. eriocarpa is mat forming, with grey-green foliage and light yellow flowers for most of the summer, and P. tommasiniana (P. cinerea) quickly forms a grey-silver mat with a show of yellow in spring. The silver-leaved tufts of P. nitida have rose-pink flowers at 5cm in early summer, and the tiny, green-leaved tabernaemontani (verna nana) has yellow flowers for most of the summer. P. ternata (chrysocraspeda) has larger green tufts and yellow flowers for many weeks, but P. t. aurantiaca is orange-buff, both at 8cm. P. t. tonguei is outstanding for its prostrate sprays of crimson-blotched, light orange flowers from clumpy plants, from June till autumn. And to round off the list, P. fragiformis (P. megalantha) has bright yellow flowers above silky, silvery foliage in early summer at 20cm.

Above: Potentilla nitida
Opposite: Potentilla ternata tonguei

PRIMULA ◑

Primulaceae

This vast genus is best divided into groups, not all of which are within the scope of this book. Most tall 'bog' primulas and the more difficult woodland or 'Petiolares' types must be excluded.

The alpine *auricula* are attractive in sun or part shade, having leathery, sometimes 'mealy' or 'powdered' leaves and heads of flowers in many colours; purple, blue, white, yellow and near red. These grow in most well-drained soils, but occasionally need to be divided or replanted more deeply. There are many under the general heading which need a mainly sunny place, good soil and drainage, but they are also suitable for troughs and an alpine house.

The 'Primrose' types, though not 'alpine' in the strict sense (except for a few very small species as distinct from cultivars) will also grow in ordinary, not-too-dry soil in sun or part shade, and make a bright display in spring. These remarks could also apply to the popular *P. denticulata*, which dislikes dry soil and which has rounded flower heads of white, mauve, violet and pink, reaching 25cm and making a splendid spring display. Another bright, moisture-loving species is *P. rosea*, the flower clusters rising in early spring before the leaves, intensely deep pink in *P. r.* 'Delight', to reach 20cm in May.

Although primulas of the 'Primrose' type are dwarf enough to use as alpines, they are even more effective as frontal supports to beds or borders. *P.* 'Garryarde Guinevere' is outstanding for its purplish foliage and lilac pink flowers. Much smaller is the tiny hybrid 'Johanna', having close rosette-type

growth and tiny, bright pink flowers in early spring. Even earlier to flower is P. 'Whitei' with large rosettes of saw-edged leaves which develop as the light blue, almost stemless flowers fade. This is a choice species for a cool, shady place with ample humus but well-drained.

All these are easy to grow, but the range needing leafy or peaty soil and shade (the woodland primulas) are more difficult to please and keep alive in dry climates and may need renewal from seed after two to three years. They include the pretty P. capitata, 15cm with powdered globular heads, and the white-flowered P. chionantha, 30cm with leathery leaves; P. frondosa, a dainty lilac, 12cm; nutans, purple, 10cm; polyneura, magenta, 20cm; yargongensis (wardii), pale lilac, 15cm; and the bright orange P. cockburniana.

P. sieboldii is more reliably perennial. This forms a slow creeping mat just below the surface and the flowers and leaves come up together in April to form a charming picture. The type is pale pink, but the clearer pink 'Geisha Girl' is better, and there is a magenta-pink 'Mikado'. The white 'Snowflakes' is very beautiful indeed, combining delightfully with Trillium sessile and Corydalis cashmeriana. These sieboldii primulas, being shallow-rooted, benefit from a peaty top dressing in late summer.

Other reliable primulas for peaty or moist soil include P. secundiflora, deep crimson, 30cm; P. alpicola, white, lemon or lavender from 35cm drooping heads, May to July; and also the relatively later flowering P. sikkimensis, which has sweetly-scented yellow bells on 35cm stems.

The above is a fairy modest selection, for the genus Primula (like Saxifraga) attracts many enthusiastic collectors who can indulge themselves in hundreds of species and cultivars if they wish.

Increased by seed, or division of well established plants in spring or autumn.

Top left: Primula rosea 'Delight'
Left: Primula 'Whitei'

PRUNELLA

Labiatae

These are amongst the easiest plants to grow, having mat-forming roots, ample leafage and a profusion of short spikes in summer. All are best cut hard back after flowering.

There are many variations of *P. incisa*, which has deeply cut, dark green leaves and magenta flowers. *P. i.* 'Rubra' is more of a reddish purple, as is *P. webbiana*, but the most colourful is 'Rotkappchen' ('Little Red Riding Hood') with flowers of deep carmine-red. All the above flower from June to August at 12–15cm, but *P.x* 'Loveliness' in white, pink and lilac shades is taller at 25cm.

Increased by division of well established plants in spring or autumn.

PTEROCEPHALUS

Dipsaceae

P. parnassi forms cushions of soft, open, grey foliage, studded with stemless, pink, scabious-type flowers on and off during summer. It is best in fairly dry soil and makes a good wall plant. Divide in spring.

PULSATILLA

Ranunculaceae

P. vulgaris (Anemone pulsatilla) is a long lived plant for a sunny position in well-drained

Below: Pulsatilla vulgaris 'Rubra'

soil. It is fairly adaptable as to soil, but is best where there is lime. The buds are almost cocooned as they emerge in March, before the ferny, greyish foliage, but open out into goblet form, with prominent orange-yellow stamens. Colours vary and may be obtained in white, pale pink, shades of lilac and lavender to maroon and red. They are generally about 20cm, but in cultivation they sometimes attain 30cm as flowering fades. The fluffy seed-heads are attractive for much of the summer. It can only be reproduced from seed, best sown as soon as ripe.

RAMONDA ◑

Gesneriaceae

These charming plants make dark green rosettes of crinkled leaves up to 12cm across, and in spring and early summer produce 10cm stems carrying lavender-mauve, golden centred flowers. They grow naturally in rock crevices facing away from the sun, and are best planted like this rather than on the flat. R. myconi and the rarer R.

nathaliae do not greatly differ and, though both are long lived, they are best reproduced from seed.

RANUNCULUS ☼

Ranunculaceae

This genus includes a few garden plants, as well as the weedy buttercups. They are not fussy as to soil, but dislike dry positions and all flower in spring and early summer.

R. amplexicaulis, best in the form grandiflora, has narrow, glaucous foliage from a small fleshy rooted plant and produces sprays carrying a few, but quite large, open pure white flowers in spring, at 15–20cm, dying back to dormancy by August. R. gouanii makes a neat green clump, bright with golden flowers in May and June, at 12cm. R. gramineus is distinct for its grassy, grey-green leaves and stems and carries a bright display of shining yellow flowers on 25cm sprays from May to July. R. montanus has a

Below left: Ramonda myconi
Below: Ranunculus gramineus
Opposite: Raoulia australis

long dormant period, but covers itself with burnished gold blooms in May, only 10cm high in the cultivar 'Molten Gold'. *R. bulbosus* (*R. speciosus*) is best in the double form 'Plenus', with very large flowers of glistening yellow, tinged green, 25cm. It likes moisture and makes a leafy clump of greenery after flowering in May and June.

All these ranunculus may safely be divided in early autumn.

RAOULIA ☼

Compositae

These form close, surface-rooting mats, almost like a film, and are of reasonably quick spread. They are best in gritty soil and full sun; and they may die out in patches during severe winters, but are easily replaced in spring. All are easily divided and have no deep roots.

R. australis is the best known for its tight mats of tiny, silvery rosettes. The small buff-coloured flowers, only 1cm high, are of no consequence, and this also applies to the slightly larger, and even more silvery, *R. hookeri*. *R. lutescens* and *R. tenuicaulis* are of more rapid growth and, with their minute yellowish flowers, good for paving and carpeting.

RHODOHYPOXIS ☼

Hypoxidaceae

These South African plants are only suitable for warm, sheltered positions, or for troughs and pans under glass. They are best dried off in winter and should not be deprived of moisture in summer. The species *R. baurii* is variable, but may be obtained to colour in named cultivars from

white through pink to red; and, although only 5cm when in flower, it continues from May to late summer. Where happy, clumps are best divided when renewed growth begins in April.

SANGUINARIA ◑

Papaveraceae

The American bloodroot (*S. canadensis*) is so called from the colour of the sap in its fleshy roots. These are brittle, but will divide with care after flowering or in late winter.

The double *S. c.* 'Plena' is the most desirable form with large, pure white flowers at 15cm, quickly followed by lobed, glaucous foliage. Its fault is in its brief display in spring, but nonetheless, it is prized as a rarity for good, light or peaty soil which is not liable to dry out.

SAPONARIA ☼

Caryophyllaceae

These have open flowers shaped like dianthus in shades of pink and rosy-red. *S. caespitosa* makes a close green hummock set with magenta-pink flowers in spring, and needs well-drained soil; as does the deep-rooted *S. olivana* which is a little taller at 5cm in a tufty clump, with light pink flowers from May to July. The best known is the quicker growing trailer *S. ocymoides*, which makes a trailing mound well covered with deep rose-pink flowers from May to August, 15cm. The choicest is a cross between the last two, *S.* 'Bressingham . This is slow to make a low mound with a display of near-red flowers, at only 5cm. It is best in partly shaded scree soil, not too dry.

Only *S. ocymoides* comes freely from seed, the others being increased by basal cuttings.

SATUREIA ☼

Labiatae

This genus has small flowers and mostly aromatic foliage. Valuable for autumn flowering, *S. montana* makes a fairly large mound to 25cm with bright blue flowers in the form 'Caerulea'. The white flowered *S. repanda* makes considerable summer spread of trailing growth, useful for walls. Both can be divided in spring.

SAXIFRAGA

Saxifragaceae

Group 1 ◑   Group 2 ◑ ●
Group 3 ◑   Group 4 ●

This large and diverse genus is best sub-divided into groups in keeping with cultural requirements based on natural habitat. Because so many varieties exist, it is a matter of personal choice.

In **Group 1** are the 'mossy' saxifrages, which are the easiest to grow in ordinary soil, but not in hot, dry positions. These have rosettes forming a low mound or carpet, almost invariably green and having sprays of open, bell-shaped flowers in April and May. Colours obtainable vary from white to cream and many shades of pink through to blood red; and heights vary from 5 to 20cm in named cultivars. 'Triumph' is a good example with a bright display of red flowers on 18cm stems. They are best replanted every two to three years to restore neatness and vigour.

Group 2 has similar cultural requirements, and includes the ubiquitous London Pride *S. umbrosa* (now *S. urbium*) which is valuable for shady places, giving good ever-

Left: Saponaria 'Bressingham'

green ground cover and a show of small, deep pink flowers on 25cm stems. This has dwarfed cultivars, such as *S. primuloides* 'Elliott's Variety', a neat miniature with evergreen rosettes and 10cm high flowers. The white *S. cuneifolia* is pretty, and there is one form with variegated rosettes. *S. aizoides atrorubens* is a slow-growing, green carpeter having brownish-red flowers in summer, 5cm high. A cross between this and *S. primuloides*, named 'Primulaize', is charming for its 8cm sprays of deep carmine from June to September. This is best in shade and peaty soil, as is the handsome *S. fortunei* and its variations. These are shallow-rooting, clump-forming plants and make a fine canopy of large, handsome leaves from spring till October, when they erupt into showers of starry-white flowers to 25cm. The type is green-leaved, coppery-green underneath; but 'Wada's Variety' has reddish-purple leaves, while *rubrifolia* is coppery-red. The last two have 20cm flowers above the leaves. Although not 100

Above: Saxifraga 'Triumph'
Right: Saxifraga oppositifolia

per cent hardy in cold areas, they are easily protected with leaves from November to March to ensure survival, and they appreciate a spring application of a peaty top dressing. The early flowering *S. oppositifolia* must be placed in this group. It prefers some sun, provided moisture is not lacking. It forms a mat of dark, sessile foliage and the terminal flowers are little cups of intensely bright pink, only 2cm above ground in March and April. It roots down as it spreads and is almost evergreen. Replanting is best in early summer when moist.

Group 3 is made up of cushion-forming saxifrages, known as Kabschias. With a few exceptions, these are slow-growing and, although they need well-drained soil, many preferring gritty or scree conditions, they dislike being in full sun all day. The easier, faster-growing kinds have sizable low mounds of mostly green or grey-green rosettes, with flowers in white or yellow shades at 5–10cm tall, often showing colour by March and continuing through April. *S. apiculata* is the best-known with primrose-yellow flowers, with a white form 'Alba'. *S. haagii* and 'Gold Dust' are deeper yellow, and 'Elizabethae' a soft yellow. There are very many Kabschias in the slower-growing range, most of them being silver-leaved cultivars having white, pink and near-red flowers as well as shades of yellow. The tiny, close-packed rosettes are hard to the touch, some with stemless flowers which are virtually at ground level, and others having short stems as a clustered flower-spike up to 10–12cm. The range includes choice connoisseurs' items which are grown in scree soil, troughs or in an alpine house. The best known of proven worth are *S.*

Below: Saxifraga apiculata

burserana 'Gloria' for a white; 'Cranbourne' and 'Jenkinsae' for light pink; 'Megasaeflora' and 'Bridget' for deep pink; 'Grace Farewell' or 'Winifred' for a near red; 'Faldonside' for lemon yellow; and 'Valerie Finnis' for primrose yellow. All flower from February to April.

Group 4 is of 'encrusted' or Aizoon saxifrages. These make rosettes mostly silvered, varying in size from under 1cm in diameter to 20cm or more with long, radiating leaves. The smaller ones are cushion-forming and like gritty but not poor or very dry soil. They also like lime as do most saxifrages, and in the wild are often found growing in chinks and crevices in limestone mountain regions. The largest, *S. longifolia* grows only in the Pyrenees in mainly vertical positions. The Aizoons are easier to grow outdoors than the more precocious Englerias. Flowerspikes arise from the centre of mature rosettes and are usually in spray formation, with a large number of small, individual flowers in white (some spotted pink) and various shades of pink. A few are light yellow, such as the green-rosetted *S. aizoon* 'Lutea' and the cultivar 'Esther'. Both are 20–25cm tall and generally this group flowers in May and June. Whites predominate, from the tiny *S. cochlearis* 'Minor' at 10cm, to the magnificent 'Tumbling Waters' at 60cm from a huge rosette. In between is the pretty 'Southside Seedling' with spotted flowers at 30cm, 'Dr Ramsey' at 20cm with white flowers, and 'Kathleen Pinsent' with shell-pink flowers at 15cm.

All these saxifrages are best from cuttings of individual rosettes taken after flowering.

Below: Saxifraga 'Tumbling Waters'

SCABIOSA ☀

Dipsaceae

Both the species below are dwarf and mounded with the typical pincushion-type flowers. *S alpina* is not very long lived, though it reproduces easily from seed, and old plants will rejuvenate by division. The light blue flowers come on 12cm stems erectly above the green tufted plants.

S. graminifolia is not only very long lived, but has a wealth of narrow basal foliage of silvery hue, making a broad mound 15cm high, just above which come lavender-blue flowers from June to September. There is a pretty, pink-flowered cultivar named 'Pinkushion' and both are very good plants, dividable in spring.

SCLERANTHUS ☀

Caryophyllaceae

S. biflorus is grown for its unusually tight, mounded cushions of distinctly golden-blue. The tiny yellow flowers are of little note, but it is a very effective plant for a trough or alpine house. Increased by division of well established plants in spring or autumn.

SCUTELLARIA ☀

Labiatae

Known as 'skull cap' from the shape of the flowers which come after the spring flush of alpines. *S. alpina* makes a surface mat of saw-edged leaves, and has 10cm spikes of pretty, cream and purple bicolour flowers from July to September. *S. hastata* grows erectly with lavender-blue flowers on 12cm stems in June and July, but is inclined to be invasive; as is the deeper blue *S. scordiifolia* of similar height. The choicest, for scree or alpine house, is *S. indica japonica*, which makes a mound of soft, grey-green foliage and has a succession of deep lavender-blue flowers at 12cm, from June to October.

All the above are easy to divide in spring.

Above: Scabiosa graminifolia 'Pinkushion'

SEDUM ☼

Crassulaceae

The name stonecrop strictly applies to only one species, *S. acre*, which, with a few others such as *S. album* and *S. dasyphyllum*, should be avoided for being a nuisance amongst choicer plants; although *S. album murale* is useful as a wall plant. Many sedums are evergreen carpeters, rooting as they spread and, with very few exceptions, all are very easy to grow in well-drained soil and a sunny position. Some, like the true stonecrop, need no soil at all.

Others form clumpy growth, dying back in winter after a show of yellow or pink-to-red flowers. *S. ewersii* has near-prostrate growth with glaucous foliage and heads of pink flowers, 15cm, in July and August; and 'Weihenstephaner Gold' makes a fine show of deep yellow above dense, green leaves from June onwards. *S. middendorffianum* is also deep yellow and neater growing at 10cm, as are the purple-green leaved *S. oreganum (obtusatum)* at 8cm and the powdery, grey-purple, mounded forms of *S. spathulifolium*, only 5cm, in June and July. *S. spurium* makes non-invasive, spreading carpets with heads of glistening pink-to-red flowers, at 8cm, from June to August. All make good foliage foil and in some, notably 'Purple Carpet' and 'Ruby Mantle', the leaves themselves are purple-maroon in colour, attractive almost the year round. The cultivar named 'Green Mantle' does not flower, but makes a close, evergreen, trouble-free carpet through which bulbs and some dwarf shrubs can grow.

Among the smaller growing sedums which die back in the winter to a compact rootstock are some that make a charming display in late summer, at about 8cm tall. These are *S. lidakense, S. pluricaule* and *S.*

Top right: Sedum cauticolum
Right: Sedum pluricaule

cauticolum. The last is a lighter pink than the other two. Hybrid cultivars from *S. cauticolum* are a little taller. 'Ruby Glow' is very showy at 15cm, and 'Vera Jameson' is of similar height with glistening, deep pink heads. Both flower from July to September. *S. tatarinowii* is a more compact and upright species with flesh-pink flower heads.

Most of the iceplant-type sedums are too tall for rock gardens, at 30–40cm, though they make a splendid autumn display. There are, however, a few with glaucous, succulent foliage and fleshy roots, which flower in spring and are not too tall. *S. rhodiola (R. rosea)* and *S. heterodontum (R. rosea heterodontum)* are both very attractive and long lived, about 25cm. *S. fastigiatum* has rich green foliage like pine needles from 15–20cm upright stems, which open to a rusty-brown flower head in summer.

The plants above are a selection from the best of this large genus, most of which are so easy to grow that they can be moved or divided for replanting at almost any time of the year.

SEMPERVIVUM ☼

Crassulaceae

Of all alpine plants, these could be said to have the least need of good soil. The name houseleek was applied to a species *S. tectorum* after it was seen growing on tiled roofs, and it is said to have some value against lightning damage.

All form rosettes, which expand as others begin to grow from beneath the lower layer of fleshy leaves. Those with small rosettes in silver, green or tinged purple will fill crevices very neatly, or gradually expand

Below: Sedum ewersii 'Weihenstephaner Gold'

into a low hummock where space permits, and they can be left to themselves for years to give year-round interest, as do all sempervivums. Those with more colourful rosettes – in shades of green towards mahogany and bronzy-purple and crimson – are legion.

They are fascinating plants to grow, and are very adaptable to pot or pan culture, as well as to many other positions where soil is well drained. They will grow quite well in old ashes and rubble; the best colourings coming when grown in semi-arid soils. In richer, moister soils they are apt to grow too lush and lose colour as well as compactness. All sempervivums, if they do so at all, flower in early summer, but in very few does this add to their attraction. Sometimes the flowering rosettes die out afterwards, but the gap is usually filled by new ones.

The smallest are those with 'spider web' filaments in the rosette, from which the specific name *arachnoideum* is derived. It has silver-grey rosettes 1cm in diameter, and deep pink flowers on 4cm stems. Three good and slightly larger forms of *S. arachnoideum* are seen in *S. a. laggeri*, *S. giuseppi* and 'Jubilee', all of which are pink-flowered.

In total, sempervivums run into several hundred, each differing in some respect, which makes them attractive to collectors who lack the means or the will for intensive, challenging cultivations as is needed with many choice, temperamental alpines. A few of the larger growing, colourful species and cultivars, such as 'Alpha', 'Beta', 'Commander Hay', 'Mahogany', 'Othello', 'Rubin', *marmoreum rubrifolium*, 'Triste' and 'Noir' can be recommended, but in recent years a host of new varieties has arrived from the U.S.A. to widen still more the range available.

Increased by division of well established plants in spring or autumn.

Top right: Sempervivum arachnoideum
Right: Sempervivum 'Othello'

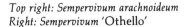

SERRATULA ☼

Compositae

S. seoanei (erroneously called shawii), although a little tall at 25cm, is included because of its late flowering and easy culture. It has deep green, fingered foliage, and in September and October carries a display of purple-rose flower heads on fluffy, thistle-type, erect stems with no prickles. Increased by division of well established plants in spring or autumn.

SILENE ☼

Caryophyllaceae

These are generally easy-to-grow plants in any well-drained soil, although S. acaulis sometimes grows in quite damp soil in the wild. The best in this close mat-forming species is S. a. pedunculata with a display of small, clear pink flowers in spring and early summer. S. alpestris forms deep green tufts and sends up 20cm sprays of white flowers, which in the double form 'Plena' are much more effective for an early summer display. S. maritima is also available in a double white form 'Plena' as well as the single; and in the pale pink 'Rosea', which makes compact, glaucous-leaved plants and has prostrate sprays of quite large flowers in summer, 2–3cm across. This type is especially good for walls. S. schafta makes very little spread and forms a neat, green-leaved plant with 15cm spikes of bright pink from July to September. The more vigorous and reliable S. s. 'Robusta' has larger flowers in a similar colour and height, flowering continuously from July to October from a steadily expanding plant.

These are all quite reliable plants, dividable in spring, but S. schafta comes best from seed. They associate agreeably with campanulas.

Below: Silene schafta 'Robusta'

SISYRINCHIUM ☼

Iridaceae

These are also very easy to grow, with a long flowering season. In habit they resemble miniature, grassy-leaved iris but in flower they are simple and open, making up in numbers for their lack of size. *S. bellum* and *S. bermudianum* have deep blue flowers on 15cm stems, from early June to August. *S. angustifolia* is narrow leaved, with light violet flowers on 20cm stems, with 'Blue Star' a very free-flowering cultivar. *S. brachypus* and *S. californicum* are both yellow, at 15cm, but the latter is less hardy. There is a white form of *S. bellum* and a white-flowering cultivar named 'Mrs Spiney'.

All the above have compact, tufty growth and, as each little fan has its own roots, division is very simple.

SOLDANELLA ◑ ●

Primulaceae

These charming, spring flowering plants sometimes baffle would-be cultivators. They demand well-drained, but not dry, gritty soil rich in humus, and shade but preferably not under trees. They form spreading clumps where happy, with a low canopy of deep green, circular leaves and dainty, lace-edged flowers dangling from slender stalks.

S. alpina is lavender-blue, spotted crimson, only 6cm high, but not so free to flower as *S. montana villosa*. This has a more vigorous spread and ample, rounded foliage beneath the 10cm, lavender-blue flowers. *S. pindicola* has more heart-shaped leaves with lilac-lavender flowers on 12cm stems. *S. minima* is

Right: Soldanella montana villosa

similar, but only 8cm tall.

Division is best in early autumn or early spring, and older plants benefit from a little top dressing to assist their shallow rooting system. They look effective with early primulas.

SOLIDAGO ☼

Compositae

As 'golden rod' these are thought of as tall border plants, but four are sufficiently dwarf to include here. One is the species *S. brachystachys* which sends up 20cm spikes of deep yellow from a clumpy plant in late summer. *S. x* 'Golden Thumb' and the similar 'Queenie' have golden-green foliage until August to September, when they open out into broad plumes of golden yellow at 25cm. *S. virgaurea nana* is a seldom seen, early flowering species which has congested spikes of deep yellow, only 15cm tall, in June and July.

Increased by division of well established plants in spring or autumn.

STACHYS ☼

Labiatae

S. nivea forms neat, evergreen clumps of deep green, crinkled leaves close to the surface. Pure white, erect, pokery spikes come from June to late summer, at 15cm. An easy and useful plant, which adds variety and enhances other late-flowering plants such as sedums. Increased by division of well established plants in spring or autumn.

SYNTHYRIS ◑

Scrophulariaceae

S. reniformis makes a neat mound of deep green, saw-edged leaves, with bright blue flowers in April and May on 10cm sprays. This is a slow-growing plant for a cool, shady place, and has rarity value. Division is best after flowering.

TANACETUM ☼

Compositae

Two silver-leaved species (sometimes listed as *Chrysanthemum*) for sun and well-drained soil. *T. densum* 'Amani' has a vigorous spread above ground, with fine silvery, filigree foliage, but a sparse show of small yellow flowers, 15cm. An excellent ground cover plant, despite its tendency to die out in patches over winter, which is easily remedied by replanting young, rooted pieces in spring. *T. herderi* is a splendid little silvery plant. It is compact growing, and has yellow button flowers to 20cm in summer. Division is best in spring.

TANAKAEA ◑ ●

Saxifragaceae

T. radicans forms a carpet of pretty greenery 8cm high, above which come tiny, flowered sprays of creamy-white flowers, tinged green, in summer. It spreads slowly from runners, and can be divided in spring; or is better left alone, if happy.

TEUCRIUM ☼

Labiatae

These are not spectacular, but some add variety to the rather sparse range of later flowering alpines. *T. ackermanii* has short, clustered spikes of deep red on greyish mounds; and both *T. aureum* (*polium*) and *aroanium* form silvery mounds with insignificant flowers. All three are about 10cm

Left: Teucrium ackermanii